Growing Up Poor

Growing Up Poor

Terry M. Williams
William Kornblum
City University of New York

Lexington Books
D.C. Heath and Company/Lexington, Massachusetts/Toronto

Library of Congress Cataloging in Publication Data

Williams, Terry (Terry M.)
   Growing up poor.

    1. Socially handicapped youth—United States. 2. Poor—United States.
3. Youth—Employment—United States. 4. Unemployment—United States. I. Kornblum,
William. II. Title.
HV1431.W55   1985   362.7′044   84-48564
ISBN 0-669-09687-3 (alk. paper)
ISBN 0-669-10277-6 (pbk.: alk. paper)

Published simultaneously in Canada
Printed in the United States of America on acid-free paper
International Standard Book Number: 0-669-09687-3 Casebound
International Standard Book Number: 0-669-10277-6 Paperbound
Library of Congress Catalog Card Number: 84-48564

To Robert Schrank and Elliot Liebow,
two who know that these are our children

Contents

Preface

This book is about the experience and outlook of American teenagers who are growing up under extremely difficult economic and social conditions. None of the young people in our study come from families that could provide them with the advantages that more affluent children enjoy. Yet although they are growing up poor in material terms, by no means are they poor in spirit. The tenacity, creativity, and hope that these young people bring to their lives should inspire the adults of our society to do more on their behalf. These are not simply the children of the poor; they are all our children.

But what can be done? Our economy is being transformed into a service and information economy in which most of the available jobs either demand high levels of education or are located at a distance from poor communities. Should government address this problem through job creation? Can we do a better job of preparing poor youth for a rapidly changing labor market? Or should private business, in partnership with government at all levels, take the lead in creating jobs and other learning opportunities for struggling young people? These are only some of the major policy questions facing a nation that at the height of its power still produces generations of dropouts and wastes its most precious resource: human talent.

Our assumption is that solutions to the problem of youth unemployment, alienation, and dependency are available. A great deal has been learned about the necessary mix of public and private initiatives. Problems of education and remediation present demographic and institutional barriers, but these are not insurmountable. The arguments that support these assumptions are not our main subject, however, although we return to them at the conclusion of this book.

Under the leadership of Congress, the U.S. Department of Labor's Office of Youth Programs, and the Ford Foundation, the late 1970s and early 1980s were marked by important demonstrations and evaluations of social programs. Millions of young people earned their first steady wages in those programs. High-quality job and training programs like the federal Job Corps were expanded, while other strategies for combining work and education were tested throughout the nation. Research on these programs and strategies generated a pragmatic analysis of what policy orientations were needed and what challenges remained. Well before the first Reagan administration took office, work was under way to develop meaningful private/public-sector partnerships at the local level. So there is no lack of experience and alternative models. And there is far less ideological disagreement than ongoing debates between liberals and conservatives would suggest. Realistic businesspeople realize that the waste of human capital and the increasing likelihood of labor shortages in some markets go hand in hand. Their interest also lies in the creation of motivated and able workers at every skill level.

What is especially lacking, however, is commitment—the collective will to work seriously on behalf of all our children. This book is a modest effort to bolster that commitment. How we think about social problems and youth—the contours of our consciousness about issues like the alienation of the young—greatly affects our resolve.

But do we really know how poor teenagers perceive the world of work in different types of communities, or how they think about personal relationships and sex, or about education and their own abilities? It is difficult, if not impossible, to take constructive action without knowledge grounded in the experiences and feelings of the young people themselves. The accounts presented in this book are a first step toward that knowledge.

We owe the opportunity to conduct this study to the initiatives and support of Robert Schrank, former program officer at the Ford Foundation; Robert Taggart, former director of the Department of Labor's Office of Youth Programs; and other members of the dedicated youth-policy network. Later stages of study benefited immensely from the help and encouragement provided by Bernard Gifford and Gordon Berlin of the Ford Foundation.

Seven talented field study directors worked for a year in communities that are home to the young people we describe. These researchers came from varied backgrounds, but all had unique capabilities for working with their specific populations. Dr. Lorraine Mayfield, who wrote the initial drafts of our material on teenage pregnancy and conducted extensive field research with teenage girls and mothers, also worked on these issues for the Manpower Demonstration and Research Corporation. Jessie Daniels of Cleveland was a seasoned youth worker, a veteran of years of work with street kids, who herself had grown up in Hough during the tough and violent 1960s. Worth Hal Thomas, who directed the field research in Meridian and the surrounding rural areas, is a dedicated grassroots organizer, civil-rights activist, and leader among the young people of eastern Mississippi. Willie Fields directed the Louisville research so skillfully that the young people of that community exhibited talents many never knew they had.

Three members of our New York City research team, Drs. William DiFazio, Jose Figueroa, and Vernon Boggs, were highly skilled and creative urban ethnographers before our study began. We simply drew upon their knowledge of the communities in which they were already living. Bill DiFazio did the research in the depressed blue-collar community of Greenpoint, Brooklyn. His voice may be heard in the accounts of young people from this embattled Brooklyn community. Jose Figueroa was already an expert on the Hispanic community of Williamsburg, Brooklyn, but our study gave him an opportunity to deepen his knowledge of the culture of Puerto Rican youth and the world of ethnic enterprise in Hispanic New York City. Vernon Boggs lent his considerable ethnographic and organizational skills to the research in Harlem, and also acted as the fiscal manager of an exceedingly complex employment demonstration. Terry Williams and William Kornblum spent their year of field research in meetings with the young people and their field study directors, and in or on the street corners, playgrounds, pool halls, classrooms, smoke shops, project apartments, parks, bodegas, garages, and all the other hangouts in the seven communities. We also spent some time in airplanes and airports.

For many reasons, it is not possible to thank the hundreds of young people and adults in the communities who helped us. We can only hope that this book lives up to their expectations. Still, there are some people whose omission from this acknowledgment would be unconscionable. McKinley Palmer of Harlem granted us exclusive use of his time during the initial stages of our research and was totally unselfish in providing us with access to key street teenagers. Margo Sharp shared her knowledge and experiences with an openness that surprised even these somewhat hard-to-impress researchers. We wish her well and thank her dearly. Dallas Toppings shared his wealth of knowledge about uptown street-corner boys and girls, and also sent us some young men and women whom we will never forget. We especially appreciate the vital assistance provided by George Unseld of the Board of Education in Louisville, Kentucky. Ronald Searcy, master teacher and administrator in the New York City school system, was as unstinting in his aid as his students were in their devotion to him.

Special thanks must go to Carolyn Smith, professional editor and tough-minded reader. Carolyn moved mountains of text to help us come up with a "good read." Our editors at Lexington Books, especially Margaret Zusky and Martha Cleary, and Roy Winnick, former publications director at the Ford Foundation, also deserve special thanks for their commitment. Aichi Kochiyama, Nina Fortin, and Nancy Naples typed and processed our drafts with unflagging good humor. Despite all this help, which gives the book its strength, we must accept any blame for its weaknesses.

Introduction: A Year in Their Lives

This book is about what could be called the generation of shrinking horizons. It tells of the lives of a sample of young people growing up in low-income communities in a society that has achieved a level of collective affluence heretofore unimagined.

The issues confronting these young men and women are not qualitatively different from those facing youth from more comfortable backgrounds. The quest for love and work, for thrills, for mentors, and for mastery over an ever-widening social world are elements of the transition from adolescence to adulthood everywhere. Poor adolescents simply have fewer of the advantages, the "social boosts" that make the quest for adulthood fun and challenging. Yet for all its similarity to adolescents of other times and places, this generation of American youth faces its own unique challenges.

If we can accept that there was a traumatized generation of Depression children in the 1930s, a scarred generation of World War II teenagers who gained maturity or found death on battlefields in Asia or Europe, a relatively affluent but anxious postwar generation in the 1950s, an embittered, floundering Vietnam generation in the 1960s and early 1970s, then it should not be difficult to accept the possibility that the 1980s promise to produce a generation of grasping competitors with narrowed horizons in terms of both mobility and ideals. In a society that can no longer sustain economic growth, the class system becomes more rigid. Competition increases, especially among the young, who must compete for a diminishing supply of "good" jobs. Youth from poverty backgrounds find themselves falling further and further behind as chronically high unemployment rates for teenagers and young adults persist. At the same time, rationalizations for a retreat from the ideals of community and equality of opportunity proliferate.

Major structural changes in the U.S. economy have eliminated hundreds of thousands of entry-level manual jobs. Mature women and adult immigrants continue to stream into the labor market. Fierce competition for a decreasing share of unskilled jobs narrows the range of opportunities for youth in private-sector employment. At the same time, skilled jobs are continually being created—jobs that are far beyond the reach of adolescents and young adults who fail in school. The prognosis for school dropouts from poor backgrounds is extremely bad. In the past they could normally compensate for school failure with early earnings at manual labor. Now they are prime candidates for depression, chronic unemployment, homicide, crime, and exploitation. We shall see, on the other hand, that despite their disadvantages there is a significant proportion of young people from poverty backgrounds who succeed despite all the odds.

There are approximately 2.5 million unemployed young people from poverty backgrounds in the U.S. population. Disproportionately black and Hispanic, even though a large numerical majority are white, they are also heavily concentrated in the nation's largest metropolitan regions, particularly the central cities. There they compound the already severe problems of an urban civic order that is deeply divided along lines of class and race.

Unemployment and underemployment of young people is one of the most serious domestic issues in the United States. Youth unemployment is closely associated with most of the nation's social problems, from drug addiction and street criminality to juvenile suicide and homicide, phenomena that reached record levels during the late 1970s and early 1980s.

Can this generation of disadvantaged youth be rescued from a destiny of street corner idleness and welfare dependency? We hope to show that it can. It is true that under the best conditions there are many who will fail for lack of innate talent and learned motivation. Yet many more who are not failing can struggle out of poverty, especially with some of the boosts that we all attempt to give our children. At present, however, the prospects of poor youth appear less encouraging than at almost any time since the Great Depression. The fruits of laissez-faire "benign neglect" and intentional cuts in youth employment and training programs only increase the chances that this generation of poor teenagers will be deprived of opportunities to achieve the responsibilities and privileges of first-class U.S. citizenship.

Among the large number of studies that have addressed this issue in the past ten years, very few have dealt with the experiences of young people in their own communities. For this reason, our assignment in undertaking yet another study for the U.S. Department of Labor was to document the life experiences of teenagers in specific communities in four U.S. cities. Our work took place in New York City; Louisville, Kentucky; Cleveland, Ohio; and Meridian, Mississippi. For each of these cities, a great deal of quantitative data on the magnitude and scope of the problems associated with youth unemployment is available. Our assignment was to employ disadvantaged youth as our co-workers and, in a year of close observation, to provide a detailed account of the lives behind the statistics in each community.

Unlike the concepts of family, career, and labor market, that of community rarely enters into the study of youth unemployment. Although the word *community* takes on important practical and ideological significance in the planning of employment programs—we hear a great deal about community-based organizations, low-income communities, local community agencies, and the like—there has been relatively little effort to view youth and employment within the context of community structure. Most studies of youth employment and unemployment are drawn from income eligibility surveys or evaluations of specific programs, in which there may or may not be some reference to the workings of the community in which youth reside. There is, thus, a wide gap to be filled. As the sociologist W. Lloyd Warner commented in his methodological note to Drake and Cayton's classic study *Black Metropolis* (New York: Harcourt Brace Jovanovich, 1945, vol. 2, p. 772):

> When a community is studied, not as an atomic sand pile of separate individuals, but as a set of interconnected human beings living in a vast web of vital relations, it is necessary to learn what the relations are which bind people together and maintain their interactions in cohesive union. This necessitates living with the people being studied, interviewing them, and observing what they do.

The methods of community study suggested in this brief passage form the basis of the work to be reported in this volume. In the course of our study we spent time with young people in at least seven communities. In each of them the experience of "community" for both youth and adults concerned with youth was the issue that guided our research. Thus, we sought to understand how racial and ethnic segregation, both as an ecological fact and as a cultural norm, influences the ability of youth to seek jobs outside their own residential areas. We also sought to understand how local community institutions, especially the schools, the voluntary civic associations, the churches, the political associations, the federally sponsored programs, and the small-scale institutions of the neighborhoods (local leagues, clubs, small business and voluntary associations) facilitate or impede the entry of disadvantaged youth into the labor market.

The choice of communities for study was made in cooperation with the Office of Youth Programs of the Department of Labor. To the three cities in which that office was most interested—Cleveland, Louisville, and Meridian—we added New York City, not only because it is our primary base of operations but because we had reason to believe that, owing to its size and to the drastic changes that have taken place in its economic base over the past decade or more, New York would add to the completeness of a detailed comparative study. The communities then would include a "world city" with an immense service economy, a midwestern city with emphasis on heavy industry, a border city characterized by lighter manufacturing industries, and a small city in the deep South with the rural areas surrounding it.

Within New York City, we selected the area of Harlem that at the time was served by Benjamin Franklin High School, that is, a large portion of lower Central Harlem and East Harlem. We also conducted field research among low-income white and Hispanic youth in Greenpoint and Williamsburg, two depressed industrial areas in Brooklyn directly across the East River from Manhattan. In Cleveland, we selected the Hough community on the city's East Side. Our research there frequently extended into the adjacent community of Glenville.

A large area of housing projects and older private houses on Louisville's West Side was the site of our research in that city, but we also had occasion to work with young people from other urban and suburban neighborhoods because of our involvement at Brown High School, the school for dropouts and special students in Louisville. In Meridian, we worked with youth and adults in neighborhoods throughout the city; our ethnographic network also extended into rural Lauderdale County and nearby Kemper County, a rural area with about ten thousand residents.

The youths' writing is at the heart of the material we present in this volume. Selections from these materials appear in the form and style in which they were written. We have not attempted to edit their writing except, in some cases, to correct spelling and add punctuation for the reader's convenience.

Our work was funded as an employment demonstration rather than as a pure research project. This meant that about two-thirds of the funds granted to us would be spent hiring, training, and working with teenagers in the chosen communities over a twelve-month period. It also meant that as a research team we would be obliged not only to conduct academic research in the communities but to do so within the context of a full-fledged youth employment program. We thus became employers and supervisors in a program that provided part-time jobs for teenagers. If the reader is interested in a more expansive version of the research methodology, we suggest reading the appended description of our methods and research experiences.

The findings of our research are embedded in descriptions of the everyday lives of young people in their communities. If we must highlight one finding, it is that in general poor teenagers seek opportunities to mature into respected adults. They do not easily relinquish the American Dream and do not fool themselves when they take routes to maturity that are self-destructive or establish them as second-class citizens. Nor do they seek handouts, even if they take them when they are grudgingly offered in lieu of more constructive challenges. Perhaps the greatest source of frustration to adults who work with disadvantaged young people is the knowledge that every day potentially valuable minds are being wasted in hedonistic escapes because more constructive and challenging opportunities are vanishing from the communities in which they work. A year spent with these young people is not a very long time, but it is sufficient to take the measure of a society that is failing to do its best for some of its neediest and most difficult children.

Growing Up Poor

1
Teenagers and Hard Times

It's a chilly Monday morning in the village of Zero, Mississippi. Ruth P. leaves her house well before daybreak to walk the two miles to the stop where she will catch the bus into Meridian. As she trudges along the dirt road that runs the length of her family's fifty-acre farm, she notices the contrast between the rows of potatoes she has already weeded and those she has not yet chopped with the hoe. Green shoots are creeping toward the new potato plants in the unweeded rows. She'll have to get to those rows this weekend, she thinks.

Between her studies at Meridian Junior College, where she is an honor student, and her work in the family's truck garden, Ruth has little time for socializing with her schoolmates. She wishes she had the time to go to parties and football games. But she is among the last of the eleven children still living at home. If she doesn't chop the crops it won't get done, and then she won't even be able to continue at the junior college. She laughs at this predicament. It seems so old-fashioned to her, so different from the families shown on television with all their cars and appliances. As she turns onto the paved road near the bus stop, Ruth thinks again how fortunate she is—at least she has many brothers and sisters to keep her company. Otherwise she could hardly stand to come home from the city to this little place so far away from everything.

In a dark hallway on 123rd Street in Harlem, Jesse, a tall, skinny fifteen-year-old, stands with his hands in his pockets. He is waiting for his "package." Casually dressed in jeans, a down jacket, sneakers ("felony shoes"), and a cap, he stands poised with a watchful eye toward the door. Finally his contact arrives and they exchange packages. Jesse gives his contact money and receives a brown paper bag. They shake hands and leave the building separately, walking in opposite directions.

Jesse lives with his parents, but he has an apartment they know nothing about. He takes the package to his apartment. There he removes an Ohaus measuring scale and a thermobar from a cabinet. He weighs the contents of the bag—28 grams of cocaine exactly (street value $1,400 uncut). He then takes the thermobar, which is used to test the melting points of various substances, and burns the powder on the bar. The bar registers 195–197 degrees centigrade, the melting point of cocaine hydrochloride. Reassured of the purity of the drug, Jesse mixes it with milk sugar (lactose); it now weighs 58 grams. The package now takes on a value of $4,200, for a $2,800 profit, tax free. Jesse is a low-level dealer in cocaine. He is also a school dropout. But he has not dropped out from work. He is working.

Daisy Alvarez and Seri Medina live in the Borinquen Plaza projects in Williamsburg, Brooklyn. The Plaza is an example of recent relatively enlightened public-housing architecture. The facades are done in warm colors; low-rise buildings are grouped around a few high-rise ones. A YMCA branch in one of the courtyards runs activities and programs for youth.

Grand Avenue, the commercial aorta of Williamsburg, is only two blocks away from the Plaza. On the weekends its shopkeepers and street peddlers do a thriving business in cheap clothing, Spanish foods, and low-cost furniture. Along the side streets, among the abandoned buildings and crowded tenements, the cash economy flourishes. Men repair autos on the street, peddle merchandise of questionable origin, and gamble in the social clubs. This is an enclave of Spanish New York; almost everyone speaks Spanish rather than English. Daisy and Seri were born in New York; they are the Newyorican generation. (Newyorican is a euphemism for Puerto Rican-born New Yorkers who speak broken Spanish and poor English and are viewed by many as suffering from an identity crisis.) They mix Spanish and English just as other first-generation youth once blended Yiddish, Italian, or Polish into transitional languages.

Daisy and Seri attend a vocational high school where they study cosmetology. They plan to work locally as beauticians and perhaps eventually find jobs in New York's fashion industry. In the meantime, however, they supplement their mothers' welfare and social security allowances by baby-sitting and running errands for their neighbors. For them the streets of Williamsburg are categorized in terms of safe and unsafe locations. The south side of Williamsburg (on the other side of the Brooklyn-Queens Expressway, which runs below grade through the community) is off limits for them. "Too many burned-out buildings and junkies," explains Daisy. "And down there by that playground on the other side of the Plaza, you don't go there at any time porque hay muchos junkies tambien, all the time," adds Seri.

Greenpoint, Brooklyn, is a turn-of-the-century manufacturing town that has been completely engulfed by New York City. In the shadow of Manhattan, just across the East River, Greenpoint limps along as a blue-collar manufacturing and warehousing center. Its economy no longer offers secure employment even to its own adult population. So the locally born white teenage dropouts are most often found hanging out in the shattered park that forms something of a town square at the village's center. The Greenpoint boys spend their days in a pill- and beer-induced haze; their nights are often spent getting into trouble with the police or with youth gangs from nearby Puerto Rican and black neighborhoods.

Eventually, after years of wretched drinking and drug bouts, after innumerable vicious scraps with other teenagers or the police, those who survive into their mid-twenties will be absorbed into the regular labor force. But it is the painful time between adolescence and adulthood that interests us here. "We see Manhattan all the time," mutters Biker, one of the Greenpoint boys. "It's just across the river sitting there, so expensive it's like you can look but don't touch. Manhattan people are different from us." Even though they grow up within sight of the nation's largest commercial center, the Greenpoint dropouts are unprepared to compete for opportunities there. Their provincialism, insecurity, and lack of education and skills consign them to wait for entry-level openings in the small factories and warehouses of their declining industrial community. While they wait they drink themselves into oblivion, always dreaming of escaping from Greenpoint.

These are four rather typical scenes from the many we could have chosen to introduce the communities and young people whose stories are told in this book. Ruth, Jesse, Daisy and Seri, and the Greenpoint boys all come from places that have been officially designated as "poverty areas." This simply means that over 60 percent of the households in these communities have annual incomes below federal poverty standards. In some ways this tells us a lot about the kinds of lives young people lead in these neighborhoods, yet in other ways it reveals very little. It tells us that the adults lack the material resources to give their children opportunities comparable to those enjoyed by middle-class children. And it signals that the economic hard times that have marked the early 1980s are felt harder in these areas than in middle-class communities. But these are only the most obvious points to be made about poverty areas and what it means to grow up in them. The differences among these communities may be more important than their similarities.

The meaning of growing up poor may be quite different for an adolescent in a Harlem public-housing project than for adolescents in industrial neighborhoods close to factories and other work places, or for young people in rural areas where work is plentiful even if jobs are scarce. These differences are referred to by the term *community ecology*. In addition, macrosocial (or *structural*, as they are commonly termed) changes in the kinds of jobs and income opportunities available in our society are experienced quite differently by the Harlem teenager than they are by the boy from Greenpoint or the young woman from the village of Zero, Mississippi. And to these ecological and structural factors that shape the lives of poor youth one needs to add the psychological and cultural aspects of life in low-income communities.

Community ecology refers to the relationships among space, population, and the material conditions of life. In earlier phases of U.S. history, such constraints played a much more determining role than they generally do today. Children expected to inherit their position in society from their parents, who in turn had carved out places for themselves, or inherited them, in the particular social order—agrarian, industrial, commercial, urban, small-town, rural—into which they were born. Today the likelihood that one will inherit social status from one's parents is diminishing rapidly. Adolescents don't know what their place in life will be. They typically experience much more insecurity about making a living than their parents did, and for the children of the poor this is saying a great deal.

There are enormous differences between the life chances of poor white teenagers growing up in an industrial community and those of poor blacks growing up in high-rise housing projects. The differences are found primarily in the fact that the white youth, especially the boys, live in the midst of whatever manufacturing and related jobs remain; the Hispanics and blacks live in extremely dense residential surroundings, literally piled on top of each other, where they must compete fiercely for all opportunities, especially the few extremely limited and marginal jobs available. Manufacturing jobs usually are located far away from the housing projects and ghetto neighborhoods.

This is only one example of how community ecology influences life chances. Adolescents like Ruth, who grow up in an environment of rural poverty, have experienced hard work ever since they were able to hold a hoe or an ax. Children from the high-rise projects of Harlem, or depressed ghetto neighborhoods like Hough in Cleveland or the West Side of Louisville, normally have no experience with work of this type, even if their parents came from rural backgrounds. Most often the children of the cities have had no sustained opportunity to work with their hands. This fact has little to do with any cultural feature that may distinguish one group from another within the poverty class. The reasons are almost purely ecological, based, that is, in the relationships between people and their communities, particularly the physical features of the area—population density, transportation systems, the presence or absence of factories, and so on.

For young people, the physical features of their neighborhoods establish the boundaries of their social universe in early adolescence. Thus, the Puerto Rican and white youth of Greenpoint and Williamsburg maintain certain streets and parks as "no man's lands" that sometimes become tragic battlegrounds. In the high-rise housing projects each building is a neighborhood in itself, often representing a maze of youth hideouts, "secret" passages, and friendly apartment hangouts. In the low-rise housing projects more typical of small and middle-sized cities, the entire project is usually stigmatized as a dangerous place, one to be avoided whenever possible. And at the low-density extreme of our study, in the rural hamlets of eastern Mississippi, young people often come to feel trapped in a world that offers few of the material and cultural values available in the larger cities or in society more generally.

Another look at Daisy and Seri will show how the community can shape its members. The girls know Williamsburg well, but they know very little about how to get around Manhattan, the center of the fashion industry—even though they hope to find jobs in that industry at some indefinite future time. This is an extremely common situation. The children of low-income New Yorkers live within commuting distance of the largest and most concentrated labor market in the nation, but limited money, fear of the city, and ignorance of resources outside their neighborhoods deprive them of the chance to take advantage of this opportunity.

The ecological features of the neighborhood establish the boundaries of daily life. Jobs and small work assignments in the neighborhood may offer young people their first earnings. The places to hang out, to compete in athletics, to mark off as turf to be defended against outsiders—these are features of the local ecology that play a significant role in the paths young people take to maturity. But the ecology of the neighborhood is only one factor in the life chances of teenagers. Of at least equal importance are transformations in the society as a whole. Changes in the economic base of the cities in which our communities are located, and sweeping changes in employment patterns, will have profound effects on the cultural and psychological conditions under which young people mature in the coming decades.

There are approximately twenty-seven million people between the ages of 14 and 21 in the U.S. population. Although large by absolute standards, this cohort of young people is smaller by about two million than the "baby boom" cohort now aged 35 to 44. By 1990 the teenage and young-adult cohort entering the labor force will be somewhat smaller—by perhaps three million—and the currently intense competition for entry-level jobs may be somewhat diminished. But this is a wishful projection, since it is based on no information about possible changes in the demand for young workers as opposed to the obvious supply. In any case, it is cold comfort for today's teenagers, who are experiencing unprecedented rates of unemployment, to know that their successors in the labor force may fare better than they. For this cohort, there is no salvation to be found in long-term changes in population size or age distribution.

In the late 1970s, before the depression in manufacturing industries idled additional millions of adult workers, the "youth unemployment problem" was a subject of concerted federal policy and research initiatives. Plans to expand subsidized youth employment and training programs called for up to $5 billion a year for a wide range of approaches aimed at helping young people make a smoother transition from school to work. These plans were eliminated very soon after the 1980 election, a subject to which we return elsewhere.

Nearly 50 percent of the eleven-million-plus who swelled the unemployment rolls in the early 1980s were teenagers or young adults. Most had never worked long enough at a steady, benefits-paying job to be eligible for unemployment compensation. But as the recession deepened in 1982 and 1983, proposed federal jobs legislation addressed the needs of unemployed adults whose skills had become obsolete or redundant, rather than those of kids with no entry-level skills at all. The new stress on providing jobs for workless heads of households threatened to leave over two million unemployed teenagers with few options in the legitimate labor market.

There simply aren't enough secure, benefits-paying jobs available today. Youth between the ages of 16 and 19 or 20 are in the least favored position in the intense competition that results from this condition, and minority youth are the most disadvantaged in this competition. The national unemployment rate fluctuated between 6 and 9 percent of the total labor force throughout the 1970s. In general, minority unemployment rates are at least twice that of the overall population. Black and Hispanic unemployment rates therefore have been fluctuating between 12 and 18 percent. And since youth unemployment rates tend to be at least twice as high as the rates for adults, unemployment rates of 12 to 18 percent are common for white youth, while for black and Hispanic youth rates of 24 to 30 percent are the norm. It is not uncommon to find minority youth unemployment rates of 40 percent or more in the nation's largest cities, which are home to millions of black and Hispanic youth. And these rates do not include young people who have at least temporarily given up the search and are on the street.

These are examples of structural problems—problems of the entire society that affect youth irrespective of the particular neighborhood or community in which they grow up. But it goes without saying that young people from low-income communities—the people whose needs are greatest—tend to be hit hardest by the lack of work and training opportunities. Every city in our study has suffered precipitous drops in manufacturing work. Men and women with years of factory experience are without steady jobs. Nor are these trends new; they were developing throughout the 1970s and are continuing into the 1980s. And as increasing numbers of women entered the labor force in the last decade, there to be joined by millions of legal and illegal immigrant workers, young people of all classes, races, and ethnic backgrounds became the least preferred job aspirants. In sum, there are a number of key social forces, operating within an ecological framework, that have a direct and often a determining influence on the chances of disadvantaged youth to find work and income. First and foremost is the spatial segregation of people and jobs. This is compounded by racial and ethnic segregation, which creates urban ghettos with their own underground economies closely articulated with the larger cash or barter economy of the more affluent classes.

Since we will have much to say about the underground economy in this volume, it is appropriate to describe it briefly here. Every community has an underground or cash economy that is vital to the survival of the middle class as well as the poor. Doctors, illegal aliens, taxi drivers, waiters, corporate executives, lawyers—all are part of the world of unreported income that makes up the underground economy. The forms or characteristics of the local underground economy vary markedly from one city to another, and from region to region. Nevertheless, the underground economy is ubiquitous. It is the "off the books" economy, the untaxed, unaccounted-for, legal and illegal marketplace for goods and services. Most young people gain their initial work experiences through intermittent labor in the cash economy. They baby-sit, do errands, sweep floors, shovel snow, garden, peddle drugs, sew, clean, and cook in a cash economy that is part of the larger adult world of irregular work.

Our study produced many youths who were heavily involved in a variety of "hustling" roles during the period of our research and afterwards. The boys had more varied hustling experiences than the girls. Boys worked as window washers at intersections, paper sellers, touts, dishwashers, fast-food cashiers, drug dealers, prostitutes, petty thieves, and con artists. Girls limited their hustling to prostitution, shoplifting, drug dealing, baby-sitting, and cashiering, and also received income from such sources as welfare, part-time work, and family members.

When we asked the teenagers to tell us what the underground economy was, they had no idea. After we explained it to them, they would say: "Oh, you mean like the numbers banker, or Mr. Ike who owns the store, or the doctor where mom works, or the mechanic at the gas station." In other words, these youth saw the underground economy as just about everybody. The words "underground economy" or "cash economy" meant absolutely nothing to them. But after an explanation was given they could recite many examples of people in their neighborhood who underreported their income. Many of the teenagers did not find this activity unusual, and they certainly did not consider it illegal. Quite the contrary, it was among the survival strategies people employed every day.

For many of the young people in our study, the cash economy is all they know. Their entire work experience has been in the hustling world. They do not see jobs in the regular economy as practical means to the ends they seek. At this point in their lives, respect, status, and prestige are achievable goals only in the illegal opportunity structure.

The situation of poor teenagers is reflected in how they feel about themselves and their life chances. "Seems like all my friends are having babies," a Meridian school dropout sighs. "Their mommas don't like it, but what can they do? Ain't nothin' else happenin' for us but babies." This expression of limited opportunity is echoed in hundreds of conversations and interviews with teenagers in the seven communities we studied. The style and themes of their self-belittlement differ: black teenagers refer to each other as "nigger"; poor white teenagers drink themselves into oblivion while blaming blacks and Hispanics for their fate; Hispanic teenagers retreat within the boundaries of their ethnic culture and question the desirability and possibility of ever becoming part of the mainstream.

Behind the manifest expressions of what it means to be a poor adolescent in a depressed community, there is a highly developed set of defenses and coping strategies. Some teenagers find their identities as members of roving gangs (now called crews), which may develop the rudiments of a retail business in narcotics, stolen goods, or sex, and legitimate acceptance as entertainers (break dancers, disc jockeys, or grafitti artists). Others may be mobilized by local youth programs that involve them in sports or cultural activities, and through which the exceptionally gifted are selected for praise, sponsorship, and further intensive instruction. The much larger number of less talented, smaller, less well-coordinated or handsome children may participate, but their sense of themselves is not to be found on the playing field or the stage. Some of them may develop a sense of self-worth by achieving in school, but in slum schools the average child is at least two years behind in basic reading, writing, and arithmetic skills. Thus, for many of the children in the communities we studied, poverty and depression are the dominant features of personal identity. This can be seen in an excerpt from our notes about a 16-year-old girl from Hough:

Elaine was released from the Juvenile Detention Center yesterday. Her release after fifteen days was finally made possible when her grandmother agreed to withdraw a PINS [person in need of supervision] petition. The grandmother takes care of Elaine and her younger sister because the mother is a chronic alcoholic. But the grandmother at seventy-two was not prepared to deal with two energetic teenage girls. She cannot offer them anything but the barest necessities of life, and she is driven into a frenzy when the girls attempt to go out at night. Their grandmother admits that she is not able to talk to the girls about these matters. They must either tolerate her discipline or leave her house.

Tall, lithe Elaine slouches in her chair, her head down, her eyes downcast. The prospect of returning to her grandmother's extremely strict supervision does not seem much better than her recent stay in the Detention Center. "It's not so bad there—at least not this time," she observes, "No fights, no funnies, and you have the stories."

The "funnies" Elaine refers to are lesbians and the "stories" are the television soap operas. Like many teenage dropouts, Elaine is hooked on television. She may watch ten or more hours per day, what James Baldwin calls escape by "TVing it." But the television only increases Elaine's depression because it continually reminds her of how much she is lacking in her life. Despite her superior intelligence, Elaine has always felt extremely ashamed in school. "If I only had some clothes. . . ." Today Elaine has come to our meeting dressed in neatly ironed jeans which are badly frayed at the cuffs and thin throughout. On top she wears a stained cheerleader's sweater, out in one elbow, which she has had since she was thirteen. Despite its holes and stains, Elaine wears the sweater every day. It reminds her, she says, of a time when she was happy.

Elaine has all the traits of an adolescent at risk of becoming a runaway street orphan or a suicide. She will not appear later in this book because, unlike the young people whose voices and stories are heard here, she was unable to sustain the attention and motivation required for employment in our project. More than a passing malaise, her depression is a debilitating, untreated illness. In the United States today there are about 350,000 adolescents with stories like Elaine's, except that they are in group homes or other institutional settings. There are another million or more whose sense of themselves is so damaged by the combined deprivations of poverty, lack of love, and absence of parental guidance that they urgently need some form of immediate care—care that will not be forthcoming unless they get into serious trouble. It is from this population that the most violent and "acting-out" youth generally emerge.

The great majority of young people from poor communities have more positive ideas about themselves and their futures. Even the most cynical, "wasted" teenagers express some belief that things will improve, a job will materialize, a love will bloom. Indeed, it is surprising how positive teenagers with so few real opportunities can be. They are living in the full exuberance of youth; with its sense of oneself as worthwhile, its positive ego strength, it is a source of sustenance that even hard times cannot fully stunt. And in poor communities times are never particularly good, so one must gain strength where one can.

Adolescence is a stage of development that parents generally fear, no matter what the family's social-class background. The years between the onset of puberty and adulthood—with its ritualized markers of marriage, parenthood, entry into the military, graduation from college, or success in holding a responsible job—these years of psychological, physical, and social transition are fraught with dangers. During the 1960s middle-class parents came to share the anxiety long experienced by less affluent parents as their children began experimenting with drugs and early sex and rejection of parental values. But these phenomena only heightened the difficulties of adolescence in an industrial society. When children begin to strike out on their own, to test their abilities among peers, to develop relationships outside the home and beyond the control of parents, all parents worry and wait for the day when their kids will settle down. In poor communities like the ones considered here, these concerns are especially well grounded. The lure of the streets and the risk of violence cannot be kept from young people who insist on making their own way to adulthood.

What forces determine whether a young person from a poor community will become a productive, literate citizen or a dependent person who seems never to be free from trouble? If we can understand the experience of growing up in poverty under a variety of conditions and family backgrounds, we can fathom the forces that act on young people to channel them into the typical life situations described in this book. Unfortunately, however, despite the frequent use of terms like "children at risk," there is no science of prediction that can be applied to the careers of poor kids—even though most of them follow rather well-determined courses from which the likelihood of major deviance is extremely small.

What are the odds that Jesse, now standing in the hallway of a Harlem drug drop, will become a junior executive in a Madison Avenue advertising firm? Probably about the same as the odds that honor student Ruth will lose her rural Mississippi rectitude and become a hootchie-kootchie dancer in New Orleans. The life course of most young people, no matter what their social class, is set by their parents, teachers, and other adult mentors. For young people following conventional paths toward achievement in family and school and civic life, individual abilities and interests have much to do with the specific opportunities grasped, but the routes taken are generally established by adults and adult institutions. Among many values poor parents cannot afford to buy, either as families or as members of communities, are supervised instruction and structured opportunities for their children—things like summer camp, music lessons, sports training, home computers, special tutoring. Instead, the majority of poor kids are sent out to the streets.

Perhaps the most basic distinction adults in poor communities make about young people in their neighborhoods or schools is that between "street" and "nonstreet." When a child is said to be "on the street" or "streety," it signifies that he or she has been fully exposed to the often violent morality of adult and adolescent street culture. To be "straight" or "nonstreet" is to have been more or less sheltered through childhood and adolescence. Like all polar categories, this one doesn't do justice to the complexity of human experience—both street and nonstreet kids may be high achievers, each in their own fashion. But for understanding adolescent life in the neighborhoods we deal with, the street-nonstreet distinction is a helpful starting point.

Many young people who do well despite their disadvantages have been more or less sheltered from prolonged competition on the streets. These sheltering experiences are generally established by adults: parents, educators, and community leaders who volunteer to work with youth in local associations. These selfless adults are responsible for maintaining the sports programs at the Y and other youth clubs. They sponsor and direct scouting groups or conduct cultural activities. They are the choirmasters and coaches and informal mentors for the adolescent generation in their communities. Without the influence of these helping adults, added hundreds of thousands of young people would be on the streets.

Some of the young people whom the reader will meet in this book, like Ruth, are among those whose maturation has been influenced by helping adults. Some of these achieving teenagers have been exposed to street influences but have chosen to pursue a course that will direct them away from the most dangerous and self-destructive aspects of street life. Parental pressure is the most direct influence toward more constructive paths, but there are kids in each of the communities who voluntarily immerse themselves in activities that will get them away from the street corners and playgrounds. And there are many others who would like to avail themselves of such opportunities but simply do not know about them or are too ashamed of their poverty to take the first steps.

The cash or underground economy of poor communities creates a wide range of sheltering experiences for adolescents, that is, experiences that provide at least some income, a sense of self-worth, and perhaps some marketable skills that can be used to gain more regular employment. But they also exploit child labor, compete with school, and are unpredictable in duration. About the best that can be said about them is that they are much better than the far more exploitive markets that create illegal hustles for teenagers and offer a readily available alternative when legitimate opportunities are scarce.

For the girls, these hustles include prostitution, shoplifting, and minor drug dealing. For the boys, they include drug dealing at a number of levels of skill and risk, number running, automobile theft, and extortion. The markets for these illegal goods and services vary a good deal from one community to another, but all hustling situations seem to share certain characteristics. First, they are based on illegal markets created and organized by adults. Second, the extent and volume of these markets is determined largely by the demand for these goods and services on the part of middle-class buyers throughout the metropolitan region. Most of the opportunities for youth in illegal hustles—especially drug dealing, which is by far the most common source of hustling opportunities—exist to serve a demand that is generated largely in more affluent communities. Without this demand, there would be far fewer opportunities for young recruits to the "fast track" hustling world.

Darryl Conway, the teenage prince of Harlem's drug world, is a unique figure. Very few teenagers who become involved in street hustles ever break into the life of fast cars and women and fancy after-hours clubs. Darryl is one of the exceptional characters who might have, in another life and another community—and with a different skin—become a supersalesman of computers or downtown real estate. Instead, he has hit the top of the much more dangerous and competitive world of cocaine and heroin deals. Among the nine hundred young people we met in Greenpoint, Harlem, Williamsburg, the ghettos of Louisville and Cleveland, and Meridian and its surrounding villages, there is only one Darryl.

Darryl's life in the hallways and clubs, Darryl's silk shirts and "bad" cars are the stuff of Hollywood exploitation movies; it is a cynical street version of the American Dream. Darryl's success creates the street myth, "I was doin' OK for a while . . . I could go back and make it." It sustains thousands of poor people of all races and background who hustle because there is nothing else that they know how to do as well.

Darryl and other less successful hustlers will explain how they got involved in the "fast track." Usually it has to do with adult influences—a "helping adult" again, but in this case the adult has selfish motives. Young people who try hustling generally have been introduced to the streets at a young age and do not have competing demands on their time. They are, as one often hears, "out there anyway, so why not try to make it pay?"

Gang activity, peer pressures of other kinds, and the urgent need for some cash all play a role in the biographies of young hustlers, but there is no generally accepted explanation of their recruitment to hustling. For example, there is no clear correlation between young people who hustle and the so-called culture-of-poverty thesis, which holds that children learn the ways of poverty from infancy and are unable to learn other, more productive behaviors. Welfare dependency, lack of a work ethic, immorality, and orientation to the present rather than the future—these are the supposed features of the culture of poverty that people born into poor households are thought to assimilate. Like most social scientists, we reject this thesis as it is applied to street hustlers. Instead, we see street hustlers using the best available means to earn income. Under other circumstances, were other, more legitimate opportunities available, the vast majority would seek out those opportunities and try to succeed in them.

Achieving in school and participating in street hustles are just two of the paths to maturity that may be followed by youth in poor communities. There are several others. Among those discussed in this volume are full- or part-time work, prostitution, membership in crews, and early motherhood. There are others, too, such as joining the Army or becoming so deeply involved in criminality that "maturity" constitutes a lifetime in prison.

These paths are not mutually exclusive. A youth who spends his early adolescence on the streets may eventually find a factory or construction job. A young woman who has been doing well in school may drop out because of pregnancy and never complete her education. There are also numerous young people who vacillate between one "career" and another. This is especially true of the Greenpoint boys, who will take a job when it is available but whose employment tends to be sporadic, leaving them free for a variety of criminal activities ranging from shoplifting to breaking and entering.

In summary, the social situations that adults create for adolescents, from legal and illegal shelters to intentional youth programs, all establish paths to maturity. The path that any given young man or woman follows is determined by a complex set of influences. The most profound is the accident of birth. Being born poor narrows life chances more than any other factor. But within the poverty class other influences are at work. Structural transformations in the economy have made urban unskilled labor increasingly redundant. The much-vaunted service economy has problems of underemployment and competition from the underground cash economy, further reducing opportunities for upward mobility for the poor in the communities we studied. And within the communities there are features of the local ecology that further influence youth. The piling up of poor households in massive public-housing projects, while it may begin to meet the need for adequate shelter, has compounded the problems of poor teenagers, who often become isolated in fortresses of poverty surrounded by economic wastelands. In the older white manufacturing villages like Greenpoint, youthful school dropouts become cut off in other ways. They feel unfit for life in the modern economy and relatively unwanted in the older industrial economy. There is little constructive work for them to do while they wait for the trickle of blue-collar chances that will eventually come their way.

As a segment of the population, poor teenagers, especially those from minority backgrounds, are in danger of becoming superfluous people. Their disadvantages make them the least competitive members of the labor force. Without special efforts to improve their basic educational level, foster their interpersonal skills, and provide them with successful work experiences, it is unlikely that they will be able to find useful roles in a society whose economic institutions are undergoing rapid change. The long delay between their last days of school and their employment at more or less regular jobs will place them at a permanent competitive disadvantage in terms of the ability to hold and develop in a secure job. Indeed, they may never find secure employment.

Perhaps the biggest difference between poor urban communities today and the same places ten or fifteen years ago is the lack of a collective initiative directed at youth problems. Since the New Deal and the beginning of state and federally sponsored youth programs directed at poor communities, untold millions of young people from poverty backgrounds have had their lives changed by such programs. Now the debate over the efficacy and morality of these programs rages again. The $5 billion that the Democrats wished to dedicate to youth programs under Carter was largely eliminated in the first Reagan administration. At this writing, the number of special youth programs in these communities has been drastically reduced. Job Corps and summer youth jobs remain at reduced or stagnant levels, but job training, youth recreation programs, and cooperative school and work programs are mostly gone or are being phased out.

"I've never seen a government program here in Hough that didn't do some good when it was going," says fiery Hough councilwoman Fanny Lewis. "The trouble is that they are undependable. Just as we know how to run them well it seems they are ending. But the programs are important, they bring in more opportunity." This is a controversial theme to which we return at the end of this book. Our viewpoint is largely in agreement with that of the

Hough leader. What is needed is a range of initiatives at each level of government rather than "quick fix" programs of the kind that too easily lend themselves to simple cessation for political expediency. But here the issue is not how to design social programs to address the problems of low-income youth. Our concern is rather for the effect of such opportunities as exist on the paths that youth may or may not take to adulthood.

2
The Superkids

> I thanked God for another day. I went to church and received a two-hundred-and-seventy-five-dollar scholarship for college. Wasn't that just beautiful? Also, I received a Certificate for the graduation from high school. (The Lord is wonderful.) I did some of my physics homework and some of my English.
>
> —Tammy R.

It's third period at Benjamin Franklin High School. Mr. C. is teaching a social-studies class. The class is composed of juniors and sophomores, about half Hispanic, the other half Afro-American. The bell marking the beginning of the class period has sounded, but pandemonium continues in the hall. The classroom is at the opposite end of the school from the principal's office. There are entrances near the corridor where students hide from the school guards to smoke marijuana. Students who are cutting class manage to open doors even after the class period has begun. Now a few have started an argument in the corridor. Mr. C. leaves the class to help restore order in the hall. He is joined there by a few of the burly school guards.

During Mr. C.'s absence the students gossip quietly. A few of the better students in the front of the class are doing their homework. The backbenchers have already put their heads down on their desks. They will remain this way unless Mr. C. attempts to prod them into awareness, a tactic he may or may not invoke, depending on how well the other students in the class seem to be responding to the lesson. The first five minutes of the class have already been lost; another few minutes will be lost when Mr. C. returns and goes over the attendance book. At the end of the class another few minutes will be lost as the students prepare to leave and Mr. C. attempts to continue teaching over this distraction.

Mr. C. returns from the hall. He is obviously upset but composes himself quickly and brings the class together as best he can. The Puerto Rican boys who sit in the rear corner of the room immediately raise a problem. One of them has forgotten his homework, but his English is so halting that the others must join in to give the routine excuses. During this exchange two of the good students in the front of the class become frustrated and complain out loud that the class is being delayed. Other students begin to raise questions about notebooks, tests, and so on. Mr. C. quickly disposes of these annoyances and soon has the students writing in their notebooks. The lesson continues, a unit on New York City government. Only a few of the students remember the names of the five boroughs, or at least not enough seem confident that they remember, so Mr. C. must review them again. The front-row students squirm with impatience. Two Puerto Rican boys are translating the content of Mr. C.'s remarks into Spanish. A radiator in the classroom begins to bang. Ten minutes before the end of the period the gym class across the corridor is let out to change in the nearby locker room. The commotion makes it difficult to hear, but Mr. C. is used to this distraction. He has already filled a blackboard with material and assignments for the students to copy at the end of the period. This gives him a chance to spend some time with the better students. Today he even has a chance to spend some time with J.S., one of the backbenchers. The boy's problem is that he has no parents and is living with friends. Mr. C. is trying to get him into the Job Corps because he is failing in school and is old enough for that residential work-study program.

For anyone who has spent any time in a slum high school this class will appear completely routine. Out of a forty-minute period, at least ten minutes are lost to settling in, getting ready to leave, and routine disturbances. Out of a fifteen-week semester, perhaps two weeks are lost to testing, special scheduling, the beginning and ending of the semester, and the like. During some weeks it is unusual to have a routine day. The concentrated rhythm of the school day is often broken by commotions, fights, and special events. Children who cannot learn at the normal pace need more sustained work on a more limited number of subjects. Yet the school is organized to give all students the same general program.

How can a student achieve in such an environment? The odds against it seem almost insurmountable, and when one realizes that many of the students have additional problems, such as the lack of one or both parents, and little or no money, success in school begins to look like an impossible dream.

But some do succeed. They are the front-row students who squirm when Mr. C. has to repeat himself. They are the "superkids," the phenomenal youth who manage not only to survive in a community devastated by crime, drug addiction, and violence, but to be recognized as achievers and encouraged to realize their potential as fully as possible.

Alain Cooper is a superkid, a young achiever who will tell his own story later in the chapter. Alain's early childhood was fairly normal, but when he was eleven his mother was convicted on a drug charge and sentenced to twelve years in prison. This is typical of the experiences of the superkids, indeed of many teenagers in the communities we studied. Loss of parents due to family breakup or early death is commonplace.

Not all of the young achievers come from broken families. Alain Cooper's best friend, Marc Gilliard, comes from an intact family of modest means. For his parents, life is a daily struggle to keep their children safe and in school. They have high standards and their children know it.

> My family is great, they praise me when I do something right and let me hear it when I do something wrong. My father always expects the best from me and if I didn't do that, don't come home. My father, who was ready to graduate when he had to drop out to take care of this family, tells me, "The only way to make it is to get a good education." Everyone in this house listen to what he says because he's right. My father always says, "Don't come home if you get left back." I never knew and nobody else knew what was going to happen if they got left back because nobody in this house ever got left back. He demands respect and gets it from all of us. He always told me, "Education first, basketball second," and still says that today. My father is one in a million because he treats me the same way I treat him, with respect and pride.

For many of the superkids this family involvement is a key factor. In every low-income community there are young people who work and go to school and fulfill family responsibilities. The largest proportion of these youths are from homes where parents have struggled for years to provide them with as many of the benefits of stability and education as possible, even at great sacrifice to themselves. The influence of family values even in the absence of material support, the relative security of religious beliefs and practice, fortunate experiences with teachers and schools—all of these factors are important in shaping the life chances of young achievers.

A smaller proportion of the young people who are succeeding against all the odds do not have any significant family resources to draw upon. Yet they manage to survive adolescence and achieve upward social and economic mobility. When one looks in detail at the life histories of these teenagers, invariably the influence of one or more adults seems to account for the constructive direction of their lives.

A major factor in the success of all of the young achievers is their own drive and motivation. Without these qualities they would get nowhere. But motivation alone is not sufficient to produce achievement. Without the intervention of adults concerned for the child's welfare, drive and motivation will be channeled in unproductive, even destructive directions. It is adult role models, together with positive values assimilated in childhood, that make the difference.

Alain's story is a case in point:

> My name is Alain Cooper. I was born on November 26, 1962 in Harlem Hospital on 135th Street in Harlem. I come from a large family. I have eight brothers and one sister. Their ages range from 23 years of age to 9 months. I have lived most of my life with my mother. At the age of three if I'm correct, my mother was pregnant with my 3rd from youngest brother, Leonard. The

event that took place at that time is one I can't seem to forget. My mother was in labor and the ambulance seemed to take forever to get there. My father had called the police who were already there. There was only one weird thing about their presence there though. Instead of helping my mother they were watching the *baseball* game on television. At the age of 6 my parents moved to 112th Street between Seventh and Eighth Avenues. I attended school regularly for the first time. I attended Public School 113 which was next door to my building. I missed very little school that year which was also for the first time. At that time in my life I seemed to live the life of an everyday little kid. I didn't know it was soon to end.

When Alain's mother was imprisoned, he and his brothers and sister did not know whether they would ever see her again. She was eventually released on parole, but "within the three years she was gone," Alain writes:

> I received an education that you cannot get from any book. I learned everything the hard way. We did not go to live with our father and none of our family stepped forward to take us. At one time it seemed as if they were auctioning us off. Everything was in a shambles.

As often happens, there was someone in the family's extended network of friends who was both willing and able to take care of them.

> Conny G. then stepped into the picture. She was only 20 years of age at the time but she was willing to take us. It was a shaky situation. There were six of us at the time in the U.S. five boys and one pregnant girl. Conny moved in with her boyfriend Junior. The two at first made a most noble gesture. Junior worked two jobs to support us while Conny worked one. Things seemed to return back to somewhat normal for awhile.
>
> Conny had a friend whose name was Jan. She was the street girl type. She was 26 years old at the time. I don't know if it was because of her influence or not but Conny was soon to become a street girl also. Things were really starting to get bad. Conny and Junior began to argue almost like clockwork.
>
> Junior then turned Muslim and that was the final straw. Conny simply refused to turn Muslim and give up her new street life she had found. In turn Conny asked Junior to leave. I had problems at home as well as in school. It seemed as though whenever someone wanted to get their kicks off they said "your mother's a jailbird."
>
> Junior left the house and it was just us and Conny. She began to slack up and eventually stopped buying food. Then she stopped paying rent. There was no reason for this to have happened. She was getting a welfare check, money from our father as well as money from dope pushers my mother knew. I do not know to this day what she did with all that money but we surely didn't see it. Conny was seldom ever home. At times she would leave for three or four days at a time. We were virtually on our own.

Alain's situation is not uncommon. The vicissitudes of life in communities like East Harlem often result in children being left on their own at an early age. When this happens, the initial response is usually to "drop out"—to hang out on street corners or in discos and clubs. This period of depression is followed by an effort to survive, one that can take a variety of forms. Frequently the kids become petty thieves. Alain, however, found a job.

> I went to work in a restaurant in the back of a bar. I was 11 years old at the time. My schedule was one that most grown people would never had survived. I woke each morning, went to school, and when school was out I went directly to work. I worked in what was once called the Royal Flush located on Lenox Avenue between 114th and 115th Streets. Surprisingly enough Conny was who I worked for. To be paid was something I never experienced. I got off work at 1:00 A.M. each night, no earlier, but sometimes later. I went home, did whatever I had to do, went to sleep and to school in the morning. There were many nights on which I would get no sleep.
>
> Conny then made one dreadful mistake, she trusted me for some unknown reason. She would leave me to take care of the restaurant. I would cook and serve the food. It was getting good for her on the street and she would leave me alone at all times. I began to tire of not being paid so I started to put the money in my pocket instead of the cash register. I had begun to learn that in this world you cannot wait for someone to give you something, you have to take it. I saw many things in that little restaurant, especially in the back. It was not unusual to see crap games with $5,000 on the floor at a time. It was not unusual to see someone get shot anywhere in the body. I've seen someone get shot in the face more than once. I learned that you trust no one at all, under no circumstances. You believe only part of what you hear and accept nothing as the total truth. One thing I learned stood out amongst everything else: grown people are carbon copies of little kids; they just take everything on a higher level. Within the course of three years I found out you have no one in this world but yourself. I became separated from my entire family and closed into myself. I became a total loner. I stayed with no one my age. It was as if I was an old man enclosed in a kid's body.

When Alain was thirteen his mother was released from prison on a special parole and the family moved to Baltimore. It was there that he met the first significant adult in his life.

> I soon met a few people who were involved with the Moorish Science Temple of America. I became interested and attended a few meetings. I soon joined the temple. The Moors were giving back all the names that the white man had given us. They no longer called themselves black, negro or colored. They were descendants of Moroccans. They professed their nationality to be Moorish American and their race to be Asiatic. They followed the teachings of the Prophet Noble Drew Ali. He stepped forward in the year 1913 to claim his people. He died in the year 1929. When he died he left R. German-Bey as

his successor. R. German-Bey was known as the Prince of Peace. I learned many things from him.

The first summer I spent in Baltimore I had a summer job. The temple was allowed one worker from the Youth Corps and I was their choice. For the entire summer of 1976 I lived at the temple. During the time I stayed there he taught me one of the most important lessons in my life. He taught me how to control myself. He taught me how to remain calm in almost any situation. He also taught me control over my body. I was on a schedule that most people in perfect physical shape could not keep up. I would run four miles every morning and seven on Sunday. I ate only natural foods, no junk food whatsoever. My head was clean shaven which kept me from sweating so much. At night all I ever did was read and study. In the daytime I practiced controlling my body. I was once able to hold my arms straight out for over ten minutes and never move a muscle.

R. German-Bey was into many things himself and one was the practice of Telekinesis. He was able to move special objects without ever touching them. He decided he wanted to teach me. One day he sent me to buy some cork stoppers and some needles. When I returned he took some paper, folded it in a pyramid shape, and sat it on top of a cork with a needle sticking up. He told me to place my hands at each side and concentrate on moving the paper. I told him I couldn't move it without touching it. He told me to just concentrate and think of making the paper spin. I sat there for over a half hour and finally it actually began to move. I became so excited when it moved I stopped concentrating and it stopped moving. I thought to myself maybe it was some wind that made it move or maybe my breathing. There was no wind in the room and I wasn't breathing that hard. I then followed the same procedure and this time it moved in about twenty minutes. That night when I went to bed I really thought about what had actually happened and accepted it as real.

Alain credits German-Bey with teaching him self-control and methods of self-discipline that proved to be of immediate and immeasurable value in his education and work experiences. German-Bey is one of several adults who have devoted special attention to this obviously bright and teachable boy. "In primary school," Alain remembers, "there was this teacher, she was a white lady, she would pay some of us to do our homework."

The desperation of Alain's preadolescent years, together with his ability to achieve in school despite his constant fatigue, created a powerful motivation to pursue scholastic excellence. When his family moved back to New York and he entered Benjamin Franklin High School, an assistant principal, Ronald Searcy, saw Alain's potential immediately. He challenged the boy to do better work at every stage of his high-school career, and encouraged him to explore the immense cultural resources of Harlem and Manhattan.

Alain's story ends on an upbeat note:

In my 11th year at Ben Franklin things were different. I began to communicate and associate with more people. It was not a large number of people but it was enough. I did very well that year in school. I made Arista and the Honor Roll.

In my senior year at Franklin I was the complete opposite of what I was in my 10th year there. I knew almost the entire school. Everything went just fine. I applied and was accepted to the Bridge-to-Medicine Program at City College. I did well in all my courses there except Physics. I did well in all my classes at Benjamin Franklin. I graduated 6th in my senior class and I'm going to attend the University of Bridgeport in September.

The superkids live in the same communities as the other teenagers we studied, but they are insulated in various ways from the violence and despair that blight the lives of their peers. Not that they aren't aware of what is happening around them—their diaries clearly show that they are—but they are able to shield themselves from the more pernicious aspects of life in their depressed neighborhoods. Involvement in family and school figures prominently in their success. So do religious beliefs and practices. In fact, for some of these young people, such as Tammy R. of Cleveland, there is little conscious division between religious and secular life. Tammy's diary illustrates this.

Thursday—Thanked God for another day. I went to school and to all of my classes. After school I went to Talis Studio and paid thirty dollars down on my graduation pictures. I gave my mother five dollars to give to my sister on her birthday which was the next day. I talked to my best male friend, Fernandez, on the phone for about forty-five minutes. I did some of my school homework . . .

Friday—Today I went downtown and I paid twenty dollars on my class ring. Today my mother gave my sister a birthday party and I gave my sister five dollars for her birthday. Today my sister is eight years old. Mother gave her a cookout party in our backyard, we had BBQ. At ten o'clock p.m. my cousin and I decided to go out dancing and we went to the CoCo. We left from the CoCo at 3:00 a.m. and we came home.

Saturday—I thanked the Lord for another day. I didn't get out of bed this morning until 9:00 a.m. I didn't do anything special today, but I did finish my Physics homework.

Sunday—I thanked God for another day. This morning I got into an argument with my sister and my mother because my sister threw crumbs on the kitchen floor on purpose and I got very angry. I told her that I was going to kill her when momma left, and my mother told me that I wasn't going to do anything to her daughter. Then I told my mother just watch and see what I do to her daughter (really I didn't do anything to her). I left home and I went to church at 10:55 a.m. and I didn't return home until 3:00 p.m. because I had an interview from one of the counselors at the church about a scholarship for college. When I came home my boyfriend, Butch, came to my house and took me to the laundrymat to wash clothes. I got home from the laundrymat at 5:30 p.m. and then I went back to church for the special program for Father's Day. I have two stepfathers and I gave them both cards on Father's Day and wished them a happy Father's Day. Also, I bought my boyfriend a pair of jeans for a Father's Day present. I read four scriptures from the Upper Room Book.

I did my English homework.

Monday—I thanked God for another day. I went to school and to all of my classes. I came home and I tried to get in touch with the interviewer at Muskingum College but I couldn't get in touch with her because she was out of town. Another woman told me that she would call me as soon as possible.

I read two chapters from the Bible. I spent some time with my boyfriend and I did a little homework.

Tuesday—I thanked the Lord for another day. I went to school and to my classes. The day seemed to me very slow because Victor didn't come to school. I worked in the office writing out high school transcripts. I took two tests in school today and I did fair on both of them. Today I signed the Seniors' Memories Books and they signed my Memories Book.

Wednesday—Thanked God for another day. I went to school and to all of my classes. I didn't do anything special, but I did talk to my special friend, Victor, on the phone. I told him I didn't like the idea of other girls confronting me or him all the time. Victor is a very handsome young man, and that's why girls stay in his face. Victor told me that he liked this young lady but she was too demanding. I asked who was that certain young girl. He said to me, Oooooo, just a certain young girl. Deep down inside of me I have a good feeling that I am that certain young girl.

My boyfriend Butch spends a lot of time with me, and he treats me like a Queen, but the only problem is that I don't love him and I have been talking or dating him over a year. I like him. Love grows so I'm still waiting.

Thursday—I thanked God for another day, and I went to school and to all of my classes. I had a very pleasant day in school. I read two scriptures in the Bible. I read scriptures in my Upper Room booklet. I did my homework. My interviewer from Muskingum called me and she interviewed me for admission into Muskingum, but nevertheless I am still going to Muskingum this summer to visit.

Friday—I thanked God for another day and I went to school and to all my classes. I worked in the office at school . . .

This diary of a typical period in the life of an achieving schoolgirl could have been written anywhere in the United States. Tammy is more or less sheltered from the vicissitudes of the streets by her religious beliefs, education, and social activities. Her path toward middle-class education and eventual employment is direct and unwavering. In group discussions Tammy speaks forcefully about how she avoids peers who use drugs and fail in school. She projects an extremely positive self-concept and is invariably selected by teachers and adults in the community for leadership roles. Here is an achieving young person whose life is singularly lacking in the influence of a particular adult figure. Tammy's life has been marked by the involvement of a part of Hough's black community that collectively shelters its youth.

There is another way in which Tammy is not typical of achieving youth in low-income communities: the direct path that her life is taking toward upward social mobility is unusual. Much more typical are the lives of children like Alain, whose escape from the ghetto depends so greatly on a combination of talent, determination, and positive adult influences.

Young people in the small city of Meridian do not differ substantially in lifestyle from those in larger cities. There is the same round of community activities, sports events, dances, parties, part-time jobs, and petty hustles. In all of these places achieving youths are able to find a peer group in which they feel comfortable and their values are supported. In more rural areas the situation is somewhat different. In small villages a child who does well in school may feel lonely and different, and may have trouble explaining to family members that college, with all its associated expenses, is important.

Take Ruth, a 19-year-old who lives on a small farmstead in the village of Zero in Lauderdale County. There are eleven children in her family. They live in a six-room house with a tin roof that has been a frequent target of high winds and tornados. The house stands on about an acre of land. The family also owns other pieces of land that are planted for crops to be used as food for the family and its animals. The children assist in planting, plowing, and hoeing the crops. Indeed, they are essential to the success of the farm, a labor-intensive operation that depends on close cooperation among family members.

Ruth might have accepted this rural life as her inescapable destiny had it not been for her father's influence. Her father, Albert, is in his early sixties. Although he has retired from active work, he still does an occasional odd job. He is not well educated, but he is a hard worker and provides for his family to the best of his ability. When one asks Ruth about her father one cannot help but notice the excitement and happiness with which she responds. "I respect and love my father for all the things that he has done for me and continues to do for me. You know, without him I would not have had the courage to seek something out for myself. Without my father I believe I wouldn't have attended college and kept my grades up. But with him I will be able to meet many of my obstacles that I have to face head on."

Alice, Ruth's mother, is in her middle fifties and is employed as a nurse's aide in a nearby state hospital. When Ruth speaks of her mother there is a look of disappointment on her face. Her relationship with her mother, she says, "is not the type of relationship that I want with my children. My mother is hardworking. We have a conversation, but not a mother-daughter conversation. Lots of things that she believes in are different from what I believe in.

"We share such values as hard work and pride," Ruth says, but she wishes she could change her mother's "dogmatic precepts and let her develop a liberal mind. If she was open minded life would be more pleasant for me, as well as for my brothers and sister."

How have her mother's precepts interfered with Ruth's life? "My mother first thought that I shouldn't go to college, but instead I should work. I tried to explain that unless I went to school, it would be impossible for me to make a decent living. She finally agreed to me attending school."

Ruth's siblings have been an important influence in her life. Her oldest sister, Mary, is twenty-five and an unmarried mother of two. When asked about her relationship with Mary, Ruth says, "We have a good relationship. Not only is she my oldest sister, but she is also my second mother. As a child she was our mother while my real mother was working. She spanked and chastised us just like my mother. Mary and I have a relationship that I wouldn't trade in for anything. The two of us are just like twins. We have so much in common." Such as? "The two of us love to talk. When you get the two of us together we talk for hours and hours. If someone else is around, they try to put a few words in every once in a while. After a short time, the person generally would just give up and listen. Not only are we able to talk, we also share a common interest and that's the Bible. We both believe that the Bible is the reason for our existence and survival thus far."

Ruth feels that she has come a long way from her childhood, when she spent many of her nonschool hours hoeing the crops and doing chores on her family's small farm. At Meridian Junior College she has been on the honor list since her first semester. Her activities in school include active participation in the forensic squad, for which she has won trophies for her interpretations of poetry and prose; part-time work as a library assistant; and membership in the school's hostess club. Ruth's involvement with her peers is limited to school hours; most of her social life stems from her close relationships with her siblings. The family network replaces the peer group in Ruth's life.

Ruth has not decided what she will do when she has finished her education. She knows that Meridian Junior College is only the first stage of what promises to be a long period of advanced education. The likelihood is that she will leave the Meridian area to pursue educational goals at a four-year university. After that her plans are still rather vague. Her only certainty is that there is no real future for her in Zero. There is simply not enough opportunity there. Although she has been extremely active in her local church and spends a good deal of time on voter registration drives, Ruth is planning to take on the larger world. But wherever she lives she will be a devout church member, and she will always return to the family homestead for reunions, for she is certain that all her personal strengths and her greatest joys in life were shaped by her childhood in a close-knit rural family.

No discussion of superkids would be complete without some mention of a special kind of young achiever: the athlete. Here is how Jamal Willis describes this path to maturity:

I was born on April 21, 1962 in Louisville, Kentucky. My parents, Mr. Kenneth Owens Thorton and Miss Elizabeth Willis, were never married, but had a very fruitful husband and wife type of relationship. My parents gave me all a boy could ask for, not pertaining to material things, but immaterial things such as love and understanding. They taught me the important factors of life, things that helped me develop into a young man.

I was never the real studious type of person, but I've always been the above average student in school. I'd receive an "A" in academics and "3" or "4" in conduct. My only reason for my conduct was that I loved to fight. Now, at 9 years of age and 141 pounds there wasn't very much maneuvering, but I could swing my arms too tough! My father used to teach me how to fight because he knew that at three feet tall and four feet wide that it can cause social problems, especially in an environment such as Parkhill, a low-income project. I went out and practiced these tactics on various young boys some. It worked on some and some it didn't. It seemed as if they were practicing it on me. I became impressive with fighting in general, so I took up boxing and indeed, it did fascinate me to a point where I actually saw a career in it.

I was chosen as one of the ten best amateur boxers to fight at Convention Center during the Muhamad Ali and Jimmy Ellis exhibition fight in March 1975. My mother was just beginning to appreciate my boxing, although she still hated it. I was injured at the Ghost Town Amusement Park in the west end. Both of my legs were almost amputated. I recovered gradually, but my mother didn't. She was already a four year veteran of diabetes and my injury really ran her down. She would forget to take her insulin, sometimes one and two days at a time. I tried to tell her I would be alright, but she'd never believe me.

She died November 9, 1975.

Since the death of my mother, I have retained my boxing ability and scholastic achievements. I have received honor roll awards since the eighth grade and I'm a candidate for West Point Academy and I held a state boxing title for two years and a national title for one. There are many goals yet I'd like to achieve physically, mentally, and socially. I find myself thanking God constantly for the many things he has pulled me through and helped me to distinguish in my standards of life as a black man, an individual and as a human being.

The young athletes may or may not do well in school. In Meridian, the main criterion for selection for summer jobs is not academic prowess but the youth's potential to be recruited to the football team of Ol' Miss. The best young football players are hired to work in meat lockers, where they carry heavy carcasses all summer—work that helps build the physique. They are rewarded for this hard work with a wage above the minimum allowed by law, despite the enthusiasm of local businesspeople for the so-called youth wage. More demanding jobs are reserved for boys who have caught the eye of the coaching staffs at Ol' Miss and its arch-rival, the University of Texas. "We keep special jobs aside for them," explains a Meridian businessman, "which we need to use in the recruiting. We put them to work on the oil rigs in the Gulf. They'll make nine or ten dollars an hour and the work will be good for their conditioning."

Whatever route a young achiever eventually takes, there is always the problem of getting through school. Benjamin Franklin High School epitomizes the obstacles to be overcome by teenagers in low-income communities. Located on 116th Street and the East River, Benjamin Franklin is Harlem's major secondary school. In 1980 it hosted a population of black and Puerto Rican children who for the most part had been losers in the competition for better-quality education. Almost half of the students came from AFDC families; three-quarters were two years or more below grade level in reading ability; the daily attendance rate was 59 percent; and the rate of graduation was abysmal. Out of a ninth-grade class of slightly over one thousand students, only 28 percent could be expected to graduate with any kind of high school diploma. And of those who graduated, only 38 percent (about 109) could be expected to apply for admission to a four-year college. The school had no laboratory sciences, no band, no college-bound classes, and no football team. It was, however, the leading basketball power in a city that prides itself on elevating that game to a high art and ritual.

It is customary to describe students in slum high schools as "alienated," and indeed the younger students who achieve two or more years below grade level and are physically lost in the crowd of older and better-known students may appear alienated because of their relative anonymity. Academic and social deficits often lead the youngsters to affect hostility and to rationalize poor performance by rejecting school values. In actuality, though, the population of so-called alienated students is quite diverse. Given improved school programs, most of these students are capable of significant improvement over a relatively short period. It is not unusual to see a student make up two or three grade levels in six months under improved conditions and with special attention. But not all students can make these gains.

There seems to be a rough "rule of thirds" in any large group of adolescents like those who attend Benjamin Franklin. About one-third of the children will be among the minority who accept school goals and whose poor performance appears to be due largely to an adverse family and peer group milieu. Young people in this group are often readily identified by teachers as "influenced by the street" but capable of solid academic success. Another third of this population affects a stance of alienation and hostility in order to rationalize the failure to learn basic skills. Very often they have never done well in school and have come to believe that they cannot achieve in the classroom. When members of this group are offered individual treatment and opportunities to achieve self-respect, they too can demonstrate remarkable progress, but the probability of success is not as high as with the more clearly capable children.

A final third of this population of low achievers are the most problematic group. They are the students for whom no amount of remediation seems to work. Emotional and intellectual disabilities prevent them from achieving at grade level. Members of this group may also be hostile or appear alienated, but more often they present themselves to teachers as "sweet kids" who unfortunately cannot succeed in classroom work. They are the most likely to drop out.

Students who drop out of school because they are unable to achieve in an academic setting are most likely to spend the remainder of their adolescent and young-adult years in petty hustles in the underground economy. Children who, with proper guidance in school-based work programs, could become productive citizens are too often recruited into the "underclass" of failures and petty criminals. Even among those who don't drop out, a large number of potential achievers simply fall through the cracks for lack of attention from helping adults. Vincent S. epitomizes these neglected youths.

> My name is Vincent S. I am 14 years old. I have 2 brothers 5 sisters 2 dogs.
> Me and my real father that died on Feb. 10, 1979 used to go to Westside Market on the Westside to take scrap metal and cast iron and steel. He had a truck.
> It was a shock to me when I heard that he died. His brother shot him over an argument, something silly and could of been avoided. Then his brother shot hisself. If his brother was still living I would shoot him dead but its a shame that both of them died.

Vincent's father was a southern migrant to Cleveland who by dint of hard work and frugality had succeeded in developing a small independent trucking business. With one truck and his own labor he made a living by hauling and carting for a number of local businesses in Hough. In the summer, when his children were out of school, he and Vincent often drove south. There they would load the truck with vegetables and melons to be sold in low-income neighborhoods in Cleveland. During these trips Vincent developed an extremely close bond with his father. When he talks about his father's death he becomes somber and depressed. Although he is fortunate to have a stepfather who loves him and takes time to help and support him, Vincent has never recovered from the shock of his father's murder and has received no special help in school or in his community to deal with the sorrow he still feels.

Vincent has, however, learned some most important lessons about working. Although his father is dead, his life is full of the influence of hardworking people. Everyone in Vincent's family works as much as they possibly can, at their jobs as well as around the house. The heroes in his life are men who work "for steel mill companies." When he grows older he would like to be able to work at a skilled industrial job, but everywhere he looks he sees men losing their jobs in the mills as a result of layoffs and plant closings. These events, like the violence around him, depress him and threaten to make him withdraw into his daydreams.

Vincent scores high on intelligence tests but is falling behind in school. Unlike Alain, Tammy, and Ruth, he has not been singled out by his teachers for special attention. Slightly built, with dark skin and a rather shabby style of dress, he tends to be shy and withdrawn despite a deeper sense of confidence and self-worth. Here is a boy with great potential to become a productive individual, but to do so he desperately needs the notice and time of adults. Right now he is lost in the crowd.

The younger girls and boys—the 13-, 14-, and 15-year-olds—are the most problematic of the achieving youths because it often is not clear if they will continue to do well. They are vulnerable to the influences of the streets because they are less job oriented and less experienced than older teenagers. Indeed, kids in this age group form perhaps the wildest segment of the illegal economy of Harlem and other poor communities.

Many of the achievers in this age group (that is, those in junior high school) appear to be hovering between careers that could lead them toward further schooling and work or toward the faster life of street hustles. They are most at risk of failure in school because of negative peer influences and the distractions of puberty. Of all the youth groups in low-income communities, this is the one that requires the most attention and resources to prevent early failure. Of course, parents generally exert the most stabilizing influence during this period, but their role in their children's lives tends to become attenuated beginning at about age fourteen, and this weakening of parental influence continues as the children become increasingly integrated into the world of the peer group.

Young people who are sure of the course their lives will take have little difficulty gaining support from such social institutions as schools and churches. They have already made their mark in school and are being selected for scholarships, summer jobs, part-time jobs, and honors. For young people like Vincent, however, the future is less clear. Vincent is typical of hundreds of minority youths who have the potential to achieve but have no special qualities that make them stand out.

Any strategy that emphasizes opportunities for achieving adolescents in low-income communities must of necessity develop the means to identify such adolescents. The highest achievers present little difficulty; one might argue that they are making their own way through extremely difficult conditions quite well. The more borderline cases present a far greater problem. Since they are available in great numbers but lack special opportunities and attention, they are at risk of never living up to their potential.

3
Working

We cannot become a nation of short order cooks and saleswomen, Xerox machine operators and messenger boys. These jobs are a weak basis for the economy; with their short hours and low pay, they are easily eliminated in prolonged downturns of the economy. To let other countries make things while we concentrate on services is debilitating. The argument that we are substituting brains for brawn is specious; brains without sinews are not good enough.

—Felix Rohatyn

These comments are echoed in numerous interviews with adults in the communities we studied. The drastic decline in manufacturing employment in most central cities has had an obvious impact on the prospects for youth in the labor market. For them, the availability of blue-collar work that promises any kind of stability is almost nil. Youth who are fortunate enough to live in communities that are surrounded by manufacturing concerns have a hard enough time finding work; young people growing up in minority neighborhoods are generally located far away from sources of manufacturing jobs.

Among the seven communities in which this study was conducted, only in white Greenpoint and rural Mississippi is employment in manual labor a modal experience for teenagers. In Hispanic Williamsburg and the black neighborhoods of Louisville, Cleveland, and Harlem, manufacturing jobs are in tremendous demand among adults; teenagers stand little chance of landing jobs in factories or construction unless—as happens in a few rare cases—a parent or close relative can provide an opportunity.

While jobs of any kind are scarce in all of the communities we studied, there are some important differences among those communities. For example, Harlem has lost most of its industrial facilities. Its residents must either commute to the city's fringe for industrial jobs or compete for white-collar work in the downtown office market. Others find work in Manhattan's vast service economy—jobs in restaurants, hotels, office mailrooms, messenger services, and the like are available but are generally confined to the secondary labor market, where advancement opportunities are few and employee turnover is consequently quite high. The garment industry in central Manhattan once hired thousands of entry-level workers each year to load trucks and push clothing racks between loft jobbers; this industry, which only two decades ago employed over 300,000 workers, now employs only 90,000. There are still jobs to be had in the garment center, but they are increasingly bid for by immigrant workers from Latin America and Asia. Young men and women do not fare nearly as well in this job market as they once did.

Young people in Williamsburg and Greenpoint, in contrast to those in Harlem, are surrounded by light manufacturing and transportation firms. Often jobs are available within what would appear to be walking distance or a short bus ride. Youth in these communities frequently do find manual labor in small factories and businesses, but the turnover rate is extremely high. And there are ecological obstacles to youth employment here too. Greenpoint youth are fearful of seeking work in the black or Puerto Rican sections of nearby Williamsburg. Hispanic youth fear the Italian neighborhoods of Williamsburg, which separate them from the other white neighborhoods of Greenpoint. Indeed, all of industrial Brooklyn is a complicated mosaic of ethnic settlements and adolescent turfs. Under these circumstances, the labor market is far from the free model of textbook theory.

Ecological obstacles to early wage employment also exist in Meridian, Mississippi, and the surrounding rural areas. Here the problems stem from vast changes in the area's economic base. The region is still going through the transition from agricultural and other primary production to secondary manufacturing that was experienced by other regions in the decades following World War II.

Since the 1950s the Meridian area has seen an influx of garment factories, which tend to locate in the rural hamlets outside the city in order to capitalize on a ready supply of inexpensive labor. The people of Meridian itself are proudest of the new Delco generator plant. This division of General Motors employs over six hundred factory workers in two plants. Efforts to attract other industries, especially high-technology industries, unite many of the city's economic leaders.

Despite the vibrancy of Meridian's new economy, marked by a thriving central business district and an influx of manufacturing concerns, the region experienced a net loss of jobs between 1950 and 1970. Adults have been forced off the land by mechanization and economies of scale, and now compete with youth for entry-level manufacturing jobs and work in the city's service economy. Even jobs in domestic service have declined here, as they have in all the cities we studied. This decline is not due to lack of available labor as much as to the combined impact of labor-saving appliances and inflation.

The opportunities that are or are not available in these and other communities form part of the context in which their young residents reach maturity. The developmental paths followed by disadvantaged youth must be understood in this context. We are dealing for the most part with cities, and with segregated communities within them, where young people are in oversupply and jobs are in undersupply. We are dealing with cities where the making of hamburgers or beds produces most of the available wage jobs, and the selling of pot or the making of babies can be equally lucrative alternatives.

Industrial society is receding farther and farther from the urban ghettos. In the few places where industrial activity continues to penetrate minority communities, one finds young people in abundance. The reader will soon meet C.J. of Scooba, Mississippi, who spends time at Grease Monkey's Garage when he is fed up with school. There he can learn some skills to help him survive. Fixing cars is something a boy can do to get by. In the packed central-city ghettos, too, young boys and teenagers hang around the garage and tire repair storefronts. Here is a little opening into the world of work, a possible way of being useful and earning some money. But gas stations and garages are not plentiful in communities where people cannot afford cars. Other city industries once had a seemingly insatiable demand for cheap labor. They brought thousands of workers and their families into the cities to work on the docks and in the print shops and on construction gangs, in hospitals and schools and small factories. Now these opportunities are shrinking in most cities.

The issue of the location of jobs might seem trivial to someone who is used to commuting to work, whether it's a short drive to a suburban industrial park or a somewhat longer subway ride from one section of the city to another or into the central city from a semisuburban residential area. But the fact is, poor youth are not mobile. Even if they can afford carfare, in most cities (New York might be considered an exception) public transportation is not geared to their needs. The mass transit system in Meridian is a case in point. It has been extremely difficult for the city government to continue even the skimpy bus transportation that now exists without a federal subsidy. "There are just too many people who use their cars," laments the mayor, "Without federal help in this we aren't going to have any mass transit around here before long." The availability of bus transportation is a vital aspect of youth access to jobs in Meridian. Our field notes are full of instances in which young people seek rides from friends and relatives. Without transportation, they are obliged to seek jobs in local stores, while the rural kids attempt to find work in the fields and forests surrounding the city.

The importance of transportation is illustrated by the situation of Mack Davis, a young man from Kemper County adjacent to Meridian. At nineteen, Mack is already well on his way toward economic independence, and his lifestyle is far different from that of the more dependent youths of the city. When Mack graduated from the small public high school in DeKalb, his father helped him fix up an old car. The car was not just a gift from an appreciative parent; it was, and is, an economic necessity. Having a car made it possible for Mack to find a job as an unskilled operative in an electric-motor plant twenty miles away. It might have been possible for Mack to ride to the plant with someone else, but because of shift changes and differences in work schedules it would have been extremely difficult for him to be certain of transportation. The car also makes it possible for Mack to get into Meridian on the weekends for movies or an occasional party. With the car, he is able to meet friends and be part of a social network of youths in the Meridian area at the same time that he holds down a well-paying job in a rural motor factory.

What we mean when we speak of "advantaged youth" often has to do with opportunities to get out of the community, to discover the larger world, to learn how to be mobile. In their early lives advantaged children typically have experiences in which they are forced to be strangers in new places. At first this comes through family trips and vacations; later it comes through summer camps and finally, by going away to college. Disadvantaged youth, on the other hand, have few opportunities to learn how to deal with strangers or "go off on their own." In school they may be taught how to present themselves for an interview and how to go job hunting, but this usually limited training can hardly prepare them to compete with young people who have been learning how to present themselves to strangers all their lives. Ironically, therefore, the children of the poor are more dependent on the limited resources of their own communities than the children of the affluent on the far greater resources of theirs.

The Greenpoint boys are a good example of this dependence on the local area. They will not be found pounding the pavement in midtown New York as youth from uptown Harlem are wont to do. When they find jobs it is generally because local employers seek white workers who will blend in well with their existing labor force. In the 1950s, when most of the fathers of these boys left school, the typical pattern was to drop out and find a relatively attractive manufacturing or transportation job. Today their sons are leaving school with the same goals, but the availability of steady work is much diminished; the periods between jobs are longer and more likely to be occupied by self-destructive and antisocial action.

Another aspect of disadvantage is lack of opportunities to be taught *how* to work. In more affluent communities teenagers who want to earn money frequently find jobs in summer camps and family businesses, or in country clubs, local offices, or industrial plants. But in the larger urban ghettos, opportunities like these are increasingly rare. There are few private lawns to mow or gardens to tend, few uncles with businesses, few local stores where the parents are special customers, and fewer and fewer local factories that hire summer help. Despite these disadvantages, many of the poor teenagers in our study groups have had early work experiences. They cook, clean, care for siblings, do errands, and work in full- or part-time jobs whenever possible. Unfortunately, the quality of their training in these "jobs" tends to be rather low.

Yet another obstacle to employment for many young people is racism and the discrimination it generates. Regina Eugene of Louisville is outspoken on this subject:

> Employment is a joke for most people and it's also a joke for me. I'm growing up in a poverty stricken area. It's hard trying to find a job. Day in and day out I'm looking in the want ads. Usually you got to be 18 years old. Most of the time, the job is in some community that I have never heard of. Every time something turns up that I'm qualified for, it's way out of my district. Once I went to a Wendy's because they had an ad in the paper. When I got there, I was told there weren't any more applications in the store and to come back tomorrow. The next day I came back and I was told the ten positions had been filled. Then I asked the man was he prejudiced. He looked at me stunned. I walked out. Finding a job is a bitch in our democratic society. Our system was designed so that everyone can develop to his or her potential, but we can't develop to our potentials because we can't get the start that we need.

Sometimes the racism is more subtle, as can be seen in this excerpt from boxer Jamal Willis' diary:

> Today is Saturday, June 8, 1980, and the weather is cloudy and hot. My brother and I had promised a friend of my aunt's that we would work out on Johnsontown Road at a festival. All three of us were to wash dishes and we would be paid four dollars an hour. We all figured that four dollars an hour would be easy money to make. At 7:30 P.M. we drove out to the festival and as we approached the driveway, there was a black security guard directing traffic. A truck pulled in the driveway with two white girls on the cab of the truck. One of the girls on the cab yelled, "Hi black cop." We knew what time it was then. We parked the car and walked back towards the festival area; by this time we recognized the fact that we were the minority of the crowd. My brother and cousin began to joke with me and said, "Look here, Jamal, if any shit starts we don't want you to start swinging, so go back to the car and pull it around; we will be there." I laughed and said "I want some of the action too." My cousin replied "No, somebody's got to make it to the car because if he doesn't it won't be just action, it'll be a massacre!"
>
> We headed for the kitchen where we had to work. My brother said "This is going to be too easy." After my brother made that statement, a lady brought in three carts of boxes three feet high. These were filled with knives and another one with spoons and the other one with forks. All of us looked at each other with our mouths wide open. My brother said "I'll wash and you dry, Jamal." My cousin had the pots and pans. After we had been washing dishes for an hour, a white lady walked in and didn't crack a smile. She had a pan of ham left from the dinner. My cousin said out loud, "Yeah, here it comes fellows." The lady made a 360 degree turn with the pan and walked right back out. Later the head lady walked in and spoke to us, then she

brought in a cart with ham and chicken on it. She told us to help ourselves and take a break. She seemed to be very nice and considerate. When she set the chicken out, she made a wisecrack about it. She said that all we have is dark meat, I'm sure you'll enjoy that.

Then her husband walked in and asked us if we had had any beer and if not, have one. I told him no thanks, but I'll take a pop. They offered us wine and beer and the father kept telling jokes and cracking piss jokes.

A thunderstorm was beginning to develop and we started washing dishes again. We looked out toward the crowd of people through a window and noticed they were evacuating the room to the fallout shelter. All the while this was going on, not once did anyone tell us about a tornado warning. My brother said that "I hope a tornado doesn't strike because I would hate to have to do these dishes all over again." Then he said, "All of these white people know that they've sinned—look how scared they are." We finished up the dishes and received our money. The father kept trying to talk black and used certain black phrases that we use. Then the father asked us back next year and we left.

Experiences like these tend to discourage black youth from finding work outside of their neighborhoods. Moreover, when teenagers from segregated communities do find work in white suburban areas, they expect to experience racism in some form. These expectations are often met. Even if the experiences are rather benign, as in this case, they reinforce the youngsters' perception that the search for work in white communities will expose them to the dangers of more racial confrontation. Thus, Jamal's friends take pains to discuss an escape strategy in case any trouble starts while they are working at the fair. The boys not only realize that trouble could easily start if the racial slurs become intolerable; they also seek to keep the young boxer from becoming involved in a fight in which he could hurt someone and cause serious trouble for himself. The fact that the boys do their work well and that they are asked to come back next year does not compensate for the racial tension they experience during the day. Multiplied by hundreds of similar experiences in their daily lives, these fleeting but negative interracial encounters discourage minority youth from seeking work in white communities.

The effects of discrimination and racism are woven throughout the life histories and diaries of all the young people who participated in our study. Achieving teenagers like Alain and Jamal agree that direct experiences with racism are not as shattering as they were in their parents' generation, but they are quick to point out the lasting effects of racism in their own daily lives. While they know that race is of declining direct significance in shaping their life chances, and that the social class of their parents is of greater importance, their strong conviction is that their family's class position is the outcome of earlier (and continuing) racism at the individual and institutional levels.

Less articulate youngsters do not separate these racial and class influences very well. They encounter racism in the social institutions that govern their lives, and they expect to experience it in their search for work whenever they compete directly with whites. "The white man is never going to give me a break" is a refrain heard so often that it becomes a self-fulfilling prophecy. One consequence of this attitude is a frequently expressed desire to join the Army. Black youth still regard service in the armed forces, and especially the attempt to gain officer status, as one of the best possible futures.

Despite the obstacles they face, a surprising proportion of poor teenagers have employment experience of some kind. Although many of them have never worked in the regular economy, they invariably can point to some work experience. These take a variety of forms, ranging from child care to working for relatives for cash. For low-income youth who find employment in the private sector, work in short-order restaurants is the most typical job experience. Alain Cooper, whom the reader met in the last chapter, had this type of experience, but more typical are the teenagers who work at Wendy's, McDonald's, and similar establishments.

Summer youth employment is another important source of early wage work experience, but as young people reach their later teens they tend to regard federally sponsored summer work programs as fit only for "younger kids." The most sought-after jobs are those that will "look good when you apply for another job." While some types of subsidized summer youth jobs fall into this category, the young people tend to feel that only jobs that set them off from the large number of youth with similar backgrounds are desirable. This attitude often extends to work in short-order restaurants.

At least 60 percent of the young people in our study had work experience gained either through family ties or in federally funded programs. Of the latter, summer youth employment accounted for by far the largest proportion of this experience. In some communities, however, and especially in New York, a large proportion of black and Hispanic youth work part time and during the summers at off-the-books jobs.

The episodic nature of employment for teens in poverty areas, even under the best of circumstances, is illustrated by Biker's experience in the job market. Biker is one of the Greenpoint boys. He quit school when he was sixteen. The work available to him at seventeen is of the type categorized by the boys as "nigger work"—a kind of work that whites, even lower-class whites, are above. They consider it their birthright to have better lives than "niggers." The extent to which they are classified with blacks in any way is an indicator of the limitations on their future. Not only does it amount to being classified with (in their own terms) an inferior group, but it is a sign of their own failure. When they are placed in special programs, either educational or occupational, that are racially mixed, it is difficult for them to face up to the fact that their position in society isn't much better than that of blacks.

Biker has been able to find work that from his point of view has a future. By a "future" he means something more than "nigger work," work that will provide the economic rewards "that everyone expects, the good life." First he worked at a chemical plant where he was learning how to use various loaders, hi-lows, and more sophisticated machines so that he could become an experienced machine operator and eventually be able to work for other companies. He would have a trade, some security, and a future.

Biker lost that job and was out on the streets again. He came to us asking about jobs, but until he could find one he occupied himself with breaking and entering (more on this in the next chapter). When he finally found another job he became very excited about it. He would be trained not only as a machine operator but as a mechanic as well. "I'm doing great," he said. "I finally have some security. They treat me great and they're teaching me to use all the machines. I could do this for the rest of my life. I'm saving up money and I'm going to buy myself a new bike."

A few weeks later we asked him how the job was turning out. "They fired me," he said. "They said it was taking me too long to learn. Not that I wasn't doing good work. They said I was doing good work but they hired this other guy, he had all this experience and he already knew how to do everything that they were teaching me how to do. They said it was just too expensive to train me to do what he could already do. So they fired me. They said I was just too expensive so they fired me. . . . Do you know of any jobs? Me and my friend bought a van together before I was fired so that we could make some extra money doing light moving. We went to every factory in Greenpoint and none of them can use us. You got any ideas?"

Two days later we talked to Biker again. He had found another job. "Yeah, I'm getting into some program. I don't remember the name of it, but they'll teach me how to become a construction worker, how to be a carpenter or an electrician. I went down with my mother today. Sounds really good and I'll get money too. Well, I got to go and get myself some joints."

Most of the time Biker is involved in the characteristic pursuits of youths of his age. He's learning Chinese kick boxing from a neighbor; he likes to get high; he regularly takes his girlfriend to the movies and dancing. Biker is a good dancer and would like to enter a dance contest because he's sure he could win. He works out with weights and swims regularly. All of these activities require money, which he gets either by working or by breaking and entering. He obviously prefers to work and understands that there is no future in being a thief, but if he can't work that's exactly what he will be.

Biker's experiences in the Greenpoint labor market are quite typical of the situation of white working-class dropouts in a period of underemployment. Biker and his peers are resisting entry into the labor force. Through the efforts of their parents, many of whom have contacts in the local factories, or else through job entry programs, they are able to find manufacturing jobs.

But as Biker's experience indicates, these jobs generally do not result in long-term commitment to wage work. Most often they are seasonal and result in layoff after a few months; but almost as often the young workers get into trouble at work because their involvement in peer groups causes them to miss work or to quit in frustration. They resist a routine of work that they are not ready to bear and are not forced to tolerate by the necessity of maintaining a household.

Not all of the teens who work are dropouts. Some, like Gina R. of Louisville, work part time. Gina, who works in a local McDonald's after school, is exemplary of the poor adolescent from a family with a thriving extended kin and friendship network. In Gina's project neighborhood there are aunts and godmothers and friends who are able to provide lighted rooms while the family waits to accumulate enough extra money to have its electricity turned on again. In this context Gina's meager earnings are not simply part-time wages that make it possible for her to enjoy life. Her wages are required to maintain the family.

Today is Thursday, July 24, and the weather is hot. Today I went to school. After coming from school I usually head straight for work at 11:00. I worked today from 11:00 to 3:00. I wasn't as tired as I usually am because I got a little rest yesterday. After coming from work, I came home and took a bath and got on some clothes as usual and headed toward the park to cool off under a tree. While I was sitting under a tree, I saw a friend pass that I hadn't seen in a while. She was taking her little girl to the pool, she asked me to walk down there with her. I had nothing better to do so I did. It was nice talking to an old friend again. After saying good-bye to her and her little girl, I came home and started getting ready for work the next day. Overall today was a good day for me. Good-bye, diary.

Today is Friday, July 25, and the weather is hot. I went to work today and after I had only been home an hour my manager called me and asked would I come in until 12:00. I agreed and went to work. There were not too many people on night-shift, only six of us and a busload of dudes [a basketball team from New York came in called the Satellites]. I knew right away they were from New York when I heard them dudes hanging on the counter saying a familiar slang that I had heard my god-brothers say: "bet-bet." There was one dude I had my eye on and wished he would stay in the back of the crowd so I could slip him my address. I didn't get a chance to, but that's the breaks. He told me he would be back the next day; I was hoping he would, too. After the crowd thinned out, I just knew it was at least something to 12:00, but it was only 9:30 and I was beat. Time passed real slow. I mentioned it to a girl and she said it takes a little time getting used to. I was determined to stick with it though because the money would be good after all the weeks of little hours.

After lots of weird and interesting people came in, 12:00 finally dragged in and it was time for me to go home. The supervisor was asking me about the possibility of me switching to night-shift. I told her I would consider it. I was too tired to make any decisions because I might regret it afterwards. In the condition I was in, I might have said anything. When I finally got out of there, I had to catch the bus. I didn't know what time the bus came, but I did know there was another one coming. The bus didn't come until one and I almost fell asleep on the bus until a girl started talking to me because they wouldn't give her any hours. I really didn't want to hear it, but I listened. I was really glad to be on my way home. All I could think about is how I was going to drag myself up at 11:00 to come to work again. When I got home, I fell straight into the bed.

Today is Sunday, July 26, and the weather is hot and humid, around 98 degrees. We owe $500.00 for an electricity bill, so our electricity is off and it can get pretty hot during the day so most of the time I'm down my aunt's house. I gave my mother some money because they haven't been sending her unemployment checks right and when she's got money she gives it to me. She used to work as a fairly well-paid secretary, but her boss fired her because she didn't come to work when my uncle died. She took the case to court because she said she was underpaid for all the work she was doing, about five doctors' work. She lost the case, but I'm sure she was on the level. Because of this me and my family didn't spend a lot of time together today or for a while past. Now I'm usually working or trying to get some rest; but right now I don't think I can rest, it's too hot. I think I'll head down to the park and check out the ball game. Later, diary.

Today is Monday, July 28. The weather is hot. Like every day these past weeks it's hot and humid again, but it doesn't bother me as much because it's only 93 degrees, and I thank God and look at myself as being blessed that it's not 100 degrees. As soon as I got up this morning, it was time for me to go to work. I didn't really want to, but I went ahead. I got to work just in time. My schedule for the work day was to cook the fries. As easy as it may seem, it's not. Today was my first time doing fries, but I got accustomed to it and was complimented on my efficiency. Sometimes I wonder why I work for a measly $12.00 a day, or only two hours a day sometimes. I think it's not worth it, which it's not; but like all restaurants it overworks and underpays. The money keeps you coming back.

For those without work, the situation is quite different. The problems of kids without work range from excessive exposure to street influences to a sort of total dropping out in which the young person makes a full-time career of partying, visiting friends, and similar pursuits. As indicated in the account of Biker's experience, the presence of our research teams in the study communities generated countless requests for help in finding employment. The following vignette from our Harlem research illustrates the urgency of these requests.

I found Anita slumped over one of the desks when I entered the office this morning. She was crying uncontrollably, but when she heard me enter she attempted to compose herself. As we talked about her feelings the situation became immediately clear. Anita is a 19-year-old woman who is working her way through City College. Her mother works extremely long hours cleaning offices in midtown Manhattan. This leaves Anita with the responsibility for caring for her own 2-year-old child as well as her four younger siblings. Often at her wits' end with fatigue and anxiety, Anita's usual calm strength failed her today. "I'm so worried about my brother, the 14-year-old. He's getting in with a rough crowd. I know he's going to get into serious trouble real soon if we can't get him into something that will help him. He's not a good student like D. [another brother]. He can't keep his mind on school and now there are these other boys who are influencing him. They've been picked up by the police a number of times in the last few months. They fight and drink and break things.

"I think part of his problem is that he's a real big boy for his age. He's strong and they look for him to fight for them. You know he gets so frustrated in school because he's always behind the others. He wants to do hard work with his body. He thinks a lot about finding some kind of construction job. He wants to become a bulldozer operator. That's all he wants, but he's only fourteen. Isn't there any kind of program or school he could get into? If someone took him and showed him how to work with his body he'd love it. Now he's just getting into trouble and driving me and my mom crazy. We could go to the court and ask them to take him away, but he's not a bad kid. They'd take him away and maybe make him into one."

Anita's fears and unanswerable questions are absolutely typical. It is probably necessary to have worked in a youth employment program like ours to know the terrible frustration of not being able to offer any real help in cases like these. Anita's brother will most likely have to get into much more serious trouble before any kind of help, even of the most dubious value, will come his way.

When young people experience long periods, often three or more months, of fruitless job search, their behavior tends to be quite similar to that of adults under the same conditions. They spend a great deal of time thinking about looking for work, somewhat less time actually tracking down leads, and increasing amounts of time doing household chores and watching television. Carol J. of Meridian, an enterprising teenage mother with an extensive work history, has provided a thumbnail sketch of the emotional cycle that teenagers go through when they want and expect to work but no jobs are to be found.

I have done all types of jobs to earn money. I worked as a babysitter for my cousin every weekend. I have cleaned homes and painted to make extra money. My stepfather was in the sodding business. I started out by stacking grass, making about $25. To me that was big money. Then I moved up to planting grass, making about $75 a week. I did that type of work until I was 14. Then I started working at a nursery.

After being laid off, I went through the following stages:
Active. When I first got laid off, I found everything to do. My time slots were all filled.
Less Active. My activities slowed down, until I was finding things to do around the house.
Bored. After I had done everything that could be done, there was nothing to do.
Depressed. With an income of $20 a week, when I was used to making about $90 to $100 a week, it made me sick. I had lost weight and had no appetite. Having to save every penny, in order to get your bills paid.
Worried. I was worried about how in the hell 20 damn dollars would take care of two people. So when I got my money it all went towards things for my son. I bought nothing for myself, except health goods.
Tried to Find Work. After making out my budget, I soon realized that I needed a job, but none were to be found.

The existence of public-sector job programs tends to keep even the most despairing young people in the job search because they provide temporary work experiences and income that keep youth engaged in the labor force. These relationships are well expressed in an excerpt from the diary kept by Madeline P. of Louisville.

A letter came in the mail about my summer job, it was just what I was hoping it would be. It's a summer reading class at Spalding College. My little sister's summer job is at the same place doing the same thing. I'm glad I won't be there by myself with all strangers. My last summer job was at Camp Taylor Elementary School, I used to have to get up at 6:00 A.M. in order to get there by 7:30. It was a real pain. I quit after I got my first check because I had a restaurant job anyway. I used to have a lot of jobs in restaurants. I quit all of them because they tried to work you to death. But I wish I had one now. Then I was still at home with Mommy.

Now I'm out on my own, and I'll take any kind of a job. At the time me and my boyfriend is looking for employment. He haven't had any luck yet, but he's been trying. He's not going to give up that easy, he's going to keep trying. I have been lucky enough to get two part-time jobs, but nothing steady yet. I am going to keep trying myself. If we both keep trying we will get one, just give it a little more time. I might go back to school if I don't have no job by the time school start. I would like to have my diploma, although my girlfriends have their diploma and still can't get a restaurant job or nothing. But it's good to have just in case you need it for a good job. You mostly need your diploma for factory jobs. I don't think I will ever get a factory job. I wish I could luck-up and get a factory job. I will get everything I want. I wouldn't waste no money, because I know how much they lay off. Soon as you start working good they're ready to lay you off. I know a lot of dudes that used to work at L&M, and Phillip Morris, that is drawing unemployment.

Madeline is anxious to work her way out of the housing project where she lives. She and her boyfriend dream about getting married, finding their own apartment, and buying a car. She worries, however, about "trouble," both for her boyfriend and for her younger siblings.

> I know a whole lot of young dudes, some of my brother's friends and some of my boyfriend's friends and also my boyfriend, that feels like if they can't get no job they have to steal, shoot craps, sell reefer, and all those other things that will get them a charge real quick. Sometimes I tell my man don't keep selling reefer because he's gonna end up in jail and he says, "I got to do something for us to enjoy ourselves. I'm doing it for you too." I told him to get up at about 7:00 in the morning and go looking for him a job for me. He said, "It ain't gonna do no good, the white man ain't gonna give me nothing." I told him it wouldn't hurt to try. We are always talking about getting us a car, both of us need a job before buying a car. We won't never be able to get out on our own unless somebody get some employment. And he likes privacy. All these things require money.

Although Madeline worked twenty hours a week for our program, she also spent time looking for other work. Elsewhere in her diary she describes how difficult it is for her to resist the temptation to stay up late with her friends, many of whom are not employed or in school.

A somewhat different outlook is prevalent among young workers in the deep South. Although these teenagers are able to find blue-collar work with relative ease, they continue to believe that there is a future waiting for them in the industrial North. Our interviews with young people in the Meridian, Mississippi, region show significant numbers of older and more highly trained workers returning from the North to their native region; however, we also found ample evidence that the lure of northward migration in search of jobs and freedom from the restraints of small-town life continues to exert a powerful influence on rural youth. This "myth of migration" is illustrated by the case of C.J., a young school dropout from the small town of Scooba in DeKalb County, Mississippi. C.J. is the oldest of eight children. He did not meet his father until he was about five years old. At that time his father came back from Chicago and his mother left with him. The following are excerpts from our field notes on C.J.:

> On August 5 around 6:30 P.M. I spotted C.J. at the corner store where a lot of the fellows hang out after work. He had smoked a joint and was feeling pretty "mellow," he stated. "Hell, what do you want to know?" We kind of eased into conversation about his childhood. He told me he loved his grandmother but his grandfather was a "mean old bastard that beat the hell out of me. My mother would come to see me and bring my sisters. We were always kind of distant and didn't say too much to each other. She would bring me things when she could. I always loved her but didn't want to stay with her and A.L."

On August 6 I located C.J. at his sister's house. C.J. was in the back room, she said. "He been acting crazy, I guess he is high." She called him and he soon appeared in the doorway half dazed. He greeted me, "Hey, my man, what's happening, I had a rough day today, them white folk worked the hell out of me today." I approached him with the idea that maybe he could find a better job. He replied, "I didn't finish no school; ain't nothing else for me to do but hard work." I asked if he had thought about going back to school. "Man, school ain't for me. When I was there I couldn't get no lesson." C.J. told me he didn't like being shut up in school. He was used to being out in the open where he could feel free. He was a troublemaker in school; he picked on the other kids and would run away to the store near the school and down to "Grease Monkey's," an old man's place where they fix old cars. The principal caught him once and brought him back to school, he says. "He nearly beat the life out of me."

On August 7 I again met with C.J. This time he was out in the yard working on a pulpwood truck. He said he could talk while he worked. After some small talk I asked him why he didn't like school. He replied that "school didn't like me. The teacher didn't like me and was always trying to make you do something you didn't want to do. Most days school was just boring. I didn't want nothing to do with it. My grandparents made me go as long as I did. When I dropped out my grandmother was very upset. So I thought I would join the Job Corps. Me and one of my friends joined and went up to Iowa. It was so cold up there and you was still shut up inside with rules and orders to go by. In six months I gladly returned home. When I got back I went to work for Grease Monkey fixing on cars. I knew something about this. Because this was where I spent most of my school days. A few months after I started work, the old shop burned down and I again was out of work. My grandmother died soon afterwards and my whole world seemed to fall apart. That old lady really cared about me. After that I moved out of town with my girlfriend Dianne."

On August 11, around noon, I stopped at the woodyard to check with C.J. I found out he had been in a fight and had gone home in a rage. When I arrived at C.J.'s house he was lying outside under a shade tree. I approached him with caution. I called out to him and asked if he was working today. "Hell no," he replied. "I liked to had to kill me a motherfucker a while ago." He informed me that he and B.G., another worker, had fought because B.G. wouldn't take his share of the work and was "always running to the white folks telling lies." He said that he wasn't going back, "don't care what." He was in a pretty foul mood, so I soon left.

On August 12, around 8:00, I went to Mississippi Wood, C.J.'s place of employment. I went into the office and talked with C.J.'s employer, who revealed that C.J. was a hard worker and that he would take him back any day. He said he understood that C.J. had not started the fight. He had fired the other party and said he was going to go looking for C.J.

On August 13, around 8:30, I circled the woodyard and did not spot C.J.'s car. I returned around noon and there were two new guys at work. I asked the boss about C.J. He replied that he had to do something because C.J. wasn't coming back.

Around 3:30 on the same day I dropped by C.J.'s place. We talked for what seemed like hours. He swore he wasn't going back and that he was leaving this one-horse town. He said he was going up around Detroit where some of his first cousins live and see if he could find a job. He said if he stayed in Scooba he would end up killing someone. He said there was no chance of him changing his mind. He told me he would catch me later on; he had to hustle up some money to get away from here.

On August 15 I stopped by the corner store and inquired about C.J. The reply I received was shocking. "Man, ain't you heard? C.J. pulled outa here last night. He said he might be back according to how things worked out. He's on his way to Detroit."

C.J. was earning $3.75 an hour at his job at the woodyard, or $150 per week before taxes. As these notes demonstrate, he had a good reputation as a worker. Even though he had experienced trouble on the job, the boss was interested in rehiring him.

C.J. knows how to work hard; what frustrates him is the thought that he will spend the rest of his life in the same community doing the same sort of work. In this respect his situation is quite similar to that of the Greenpoint boys, but C.J. does not care to get involved in street hustling. "I believe," he explains, "that I can make more working on a job. I'm not good at hustling. I been out there and it ain't nothing but trouble." C.J. chose to try his luck in Detroit because he has some kin there. He did not try nearby Birmingham, Alabama, because he knows that the manufacturing industry there is extremely depressed. Nor did he opt for migration westward to Texas, where jobs are supposedly more plentiful, because he had no one to stay with there. His family history is linked to the great northward migration of blacks. C.J. knows that the economic situation of his people in the northern industrial cities is not good, but like millions of young black men before him, he hopes that he will be lucky.

The demand side of the youth employment picture is not encouraging in any of the communities we studied. But the contours of the labor market are only part of the story. In New York, where the labor market is large even with recent job losses, there are almost always jobs for highly motivated young people. Although the overall market is not able to absorb the number of youths who register with state employment services, a young person who seriously seeks work will eventually find it. This is not as true in Cleveland or Louisville, and certainly not in Meridian. But even in these small cities a highly motivated young person can find work even if the overall number of openings would not be sufficient without significant government work subsidies. This quite obvious fact calls attention to the controlling presence of parents and other adults in the lives of young people. More than that, it is an indication of the crucial role of the public sector in youth employment.

In smaller cities like Louisville, there is no large central-city labor market capable of absorbing thousands of youthful job seekers. Nor are the ghetto neighborhoods in these cities surrounded by industrial concerns, as is the case in Greenpoint and Williamsburg. This ecological fact tends to make the youth in minority neighborhoods almost entirely dependent on jobs available in the public sector through summer youth employment and other federally sponsored programs.

In the course of our research we encountered every existing youth manpower program, from Job Corps and Cooperative Work Study to Youth Employment and Demonstration Projects Acts (YEDPA) and Comprehensive Employment Training Act (CETA) youth programs to basic summer youth employment. In Cleveland, Tammy and Vincent found summer jobs with the city's summer youth employment program. So did most of the young people we met there. Vincent was assigned to an outdoor work crew of about twenty boys who spent their eight weeks of employment in the cemeteries and parks of Cleveland's East Side. Their work consisted of trimming grass and bushes, cleaning clogged drains, and a great deal of weeding. Tammy worked with two other girls her age in her church's enrichment program for young people. She helped take children on field trips. In Louisville, Jamal was hired by his Boys Club to assist the club supervisor in a variety of tasks ranging from teaching assistance in the sports program to general housekeeping in the locker rooms. In Harlem, Alain worked two summers for a community theater organization. He counts this as one of the most important work experiences of his life. At the theater he was exposed to black intellectuals and artists, people who reinforced his determination to take school seriously. Many of Alain's peers found summer jobs with the Harlem Rucker League. They learned to officiate at basketball games, keep time, record scores, and manage schedules.

It is important to note that low-income minority families depend on federally subsidized jobs as a source of income to allow the teenagers to resume schooling in the fall with some new clothes and supplies. Summer work also permits poor teenagers to enjoy some of the pleasures that are taken for granted by more affluent adolescents. It also, of course, contributes to the family budget. Subsidized work, especially in summer work programs, has become an integral aspect of the survival system of low-income neighborhoods. The private sector is simply too weak or too distant to make adequate work experiences available.

Despite these well-known facts, funding for subsidized jobs has been cut drastically under the present administration. Part of the rationale for the cuts is that the jobs provided are of the "make-work" variety and that they produce no long-term benefits either to the worker or to the community. We will have more to say about these claims in a later chapter. Here it will suffice to take a brief look at one youth's experience in a subsidized job.

Vincent's work experience was largely positive. The work in the cemetery could be physically taxing, but it made him "feel like a man." The chief
difficulty he experienced was that most of his peers on the job did not share
his enthusiasm. The other boys had no previous experience with manual
labor. Nor had any systematic effort been made to teach them how to work
with the simple tools they were given. Rakes and shovels are not as familiar
to boys who have grown up in Hough as they tend to be to young people who
find similar work in Meridian and the surrounding villages. In the following
excerpt from Vincent's diary their lack of interest in the work is evident.

> Today at the Woodland graveyard we used a Toro weedeater. We started
> cutting weeds. There were many mosquitos where we were working at. Then
> we were working on the truck in the graveyard. We had to pick up leaves and
> put them on the truck. We kept on getting bit by mosquitos. Then we went
> down to the other half of the graveyard to pick up bushes and trees, we had
> to fill up the truck two times, then we would be through. The driver of the
> truck bought two quarts of Old English beer. They passed the beer toward
> me and I said go ahead, I don't drink. Then they started calling me a square.
> I said just because you all drink doesn't mean that I have to drink. The driver
> of the truck said he's right, just drink the beer if you want some and don't
> worry about no one else but yourself. So then one boy who worked on the
> truck lit up a stick or a joint or whatever they call it or reefer. So before they
> passed it to me I told them that I don't smoke, either, so don't pass it to me.

When the boys in the Hough cemetery avoid work by hiding in the
bushes and smoking pot, Vincent feels ashamed of them. He wishes he could
be working side by side with his father again. There would be no pressure to
go easy and make the work last. The job would need to be finished so that the
next one could begin. What Vincent does not understand is that no matter
what their age and experience, workers everywhere seek to maximize their
autonomy at work. This means that they seek to put in an amount of effort
that seems acceptable to their supervisors over time. When they are not
engaged in active efforts to meet formal or informal production goals,
workers pride themselves on finding creative ways to enjoy some leisure while
on the job. What often happens in summer work programs, however, is that
workers who are already stigmatized for being young, for their minority identity, and for working on public employment are further stigmatized by their
relatively unsophisticated attempts to behave the way workers do in every
culture.

It has become fashionable to compare U.S. workers with those in Japan,
who seem not to shirk on the job. A full review of this comparison is beyond
the scope of this discussion, but the issue is relevant because summer youth
workers tend to be judged against highly idealized standards. In the press and
in casual evaluations of summer work, youthful workers are generally por-

trayed as performing unnecessary work that is poorly supervised and at which there is a great deal of sloughing off. The experiences of the young people themselves as recorded in their notes and in our own experience as supervisors lead one to a more sophisticated evaluation.

When a young person is employed as an individual rather than as part of a work gang, the quality of the work experience and the actual work performed is a matter of the youth's capabilities as well as the quality of the supervision the worker receives on the job. The more that supervision can be characterized as a mentor relationship, the greater the gains by the young worker in terms of positive attitudes toward work, ability to perform at acceptable levels, and enhanced employability. Where youths work in crews or work gangs, on the other hand, it is much more difficult for these ends to be met. This is not to say that there are not many instances in which young people working in teams make gains similar to those often encountered in more individual employee-supervisor situations, but the dominant experience of teenagers working in large groups tends to be much more problematic.

Our view of the importance of employment opportunities for youth also takes into consideration the influence of unemployed teenagers on those who work. While Alain, Tammy, Vincent, Jamal, and the majority of the other young people with whom we worked in over eighteen months of field research were seeking jobs through summer youth employment or other federally subsidized work, many of their brothers and sisters were simply hanging out. They were unable to find jobs because they began the search too late, did not know where and how to secure the work, or simply preferred to be unemployed. This last category is extremely small. Given a concrete opportunity to work, it is a rare low-income teenager who will not take the job. Those who do not are the nucleus of the future population of street corner people. They will influence other young people in their communities who do not find jobs. The expense of this negative influence needs to be calculated in any realistic reckoning of the cost of subsidized work.

says one, "how much is it?" "Three and a quarter." "No, no, then gimme the other one. Why is it that much?" "That's just what it is." "Forget it."

This is the exception that proves the rule. Most of the time needles sell like gold futures on the stock market. The neighborhood once was flooded with junkies, but it is changing slowly. The candy store is one of the last institutions in the area to serve this particular consumer group. In fact, the store operates on several levels. It's a hangout for kids, number runners, drug dealers, and winos. The kids can buy reefer; adults can buy wine under the counter; boosters (sellers of stolen goods) sell their wares to customers and managers alike. The store has two phones that are constantly ringing, and a high plastic shield to prevent robberies. A cut-out cardboard box under the phones serves for waste disposal.

Several teenagers are standing around in the store, wearing sneakers and "pirate" caps turned "ace, deuce, trey" (to the side). One of them, C.C., is a sometime student at Fashion Industry High School downtown. He says he likes the school because there are so many girls in his classes. "School's OK, but it ain't no money in going to school. I need a job," he adds.

C.C. and the others are too young to remember the Seventh Avenue of 1964, the year thousands of Harlem residents rioted over the death of James Powell, a 15-year-old black who had been killed by a white police officer. Most of them won't remember Malcolm X standing on the corner of Seventh and 125th Street delivering eloquent speeches about racism, discrimination, and inhumanity in the United States. Nor will they remember Minton's, the famous jazz club that once stood across the street from the candy store. It was at Minton's that Charlie Parker, Dizzy Gillespie, Roy Eldridge, and many other jazz greats held jam sessions until the early morning hours.

Seventh was the avenue of the big-time hustlers. There they sported their fine cars and pretty women. There Nicky Barnes, Tony Rome, Pee Wee Chatwick, the Cisco Kid, Goldfinger, and other fast-track hustlers made fortunes. To today's kids they are folk heros. The names of infamous street hustlers who made it into the big time are given legendary status; the kids hope to stand in their ranks some day.

C.C. has a long way to go if he wants to make it to the big time. Right now all he can do is talk big. Wearing a floppy hat that he claims is a Christian Dior, a fur-type vest, sneakers, and khaki trousers, he takes a perverse pleasure in shouting obscenities at his peers. As one of them, Zero, dressed in a grey hooded jacked zipped up to the neck, passes to go into the store, C.C. looks at him.

"Yo, what you wearing all of that shit for? This ain't the north pole—you look like a motherfucking polar bear. Why don't you take off some of them clothes, you overdressed motherfucker?"

Zero gets to the door, steps in for a second, then comes out, grabs C.C. round the neck, and proceeds to twist his head around. As he twists he

4
On the Streets

interesting

> My idol was Watusi. He had the Cadillac and the
> man, I wanted to be like him if I had to die trying
> one out there, though. Besides Movie Star and
> Nicky Barnes, Mustache Billy, Bobby Whiteboy, G
> bie, Tony Rome, and a whole lot of others. Watus
> lieutenants. I was excited by all of that. I wanted
> the fancy cars. I wanted to dress good. And you
> dressing. In order to get those things you had t
> money. My family couldn't afford to pay that ki
> clothes—you know, my mother was on welfare
> well, somewhere on something else. So you more
> on your own. So I started getting mine early.

I t's a chilly October evening in Harlem. On 118th Street
nue every other building is either bricked up, abandone
occupied. The neighborhood to the east is in rapid tr
available housing stock is decreasing rapidly. There are tw
the area, though. Harlem World, a huge disco (claimed
largest), is located on 116th Street across from the Muslim
new complex that caters to teenagers and young adults. The
is the conversion of Graham Court, an elegant landmark t
of the black elite in the 1920s, 1930s, and 1940s. It is bei
cooperative housing, with many poets, writers, painters, do
among its tenants. There are several new shops on the block
store, a hardware store, a new restaurant, and new hous
under construction. These signs of vitality appear in sharp
employed teenagers who sit and stand and rap on the cor
the area.

The candy store on 118th Street and Seventh Avenue i
hours a day, seven days a week. In the tradition of the
wagon, it dispenses bootleg alcohol, marijuana joints, bag
cut drugs, and advice on life, crime, and the latest number,
selection of household items. Tonight the store is filled
many with their wrists swollen and scarred by injections
who come into the store are junkies or ex-junkies. "Gimme

mumbles something like "I-done-told-you-to-stop-fucking-with-me-ain't-I? But-you-keep-on-fucking-with-me-don'tcha?"

"Let me go, Zero—let me go!"

As soon as he is released C.C. shouts angrily, "I'm gonna fuck you up, Zero. Wait and see." He looks in the trash cans for something to hit Zero with. Finding nothing, he comes over and pushes him. Zero pushes him away. After much blustering and panting—"I'm gonna fuck you up, you longheaded motherfucker"—C.C. finds a bottle, breaks it on the concrete in classic Hollywood style, and comes dangerously close to cutting Zero's face and throat. One of the men who buy the syringes from the store happens down the street and attempts to hold Zero off, but now Zero seems more reluctant to move on C.C. "Walk, little one," the junkie says to C.C., "Why don't you walk? Why you keep on doing this? Go on and leave this cat alone. Why don't you walk, man? Even a fool knows when to walk."

"No, I ain't gonna go nowhere." C.C. is almost crying. "I'm on this block all the time and I ain't gonna run nowhere."

"I got a piece [gun] that will take care of you if you think you bad," Zero reminds him. "Don't you forget that."

"Ah, fuck you, motherfucker."

C.C. and Zero are among the countless youth who are on the streets because they have dropped out of school, cannot find jobs, or both. When they aren't hanging out at the candy store or trying to kill each other, they spend their time stealing bicycles or engaging in petty hustles of various kinds, including doing favors for more successful hustlers. They are among the losers of the street world. Darryl Conway is one of the winners.

At five feet nine, Darryl is rather short, well built but not muscular. He is intense but has a quick smile. He has always been a play maker with the basketball and is considered "death" on the court. While he dresses stylishly, he avoids "flash" and can often be seen in jeans and sneakers.

Darryl's expensive tastes are evident in his wardrobe—a mink coat, several pairs of three-hundred-dollar boots, a closet filled with silk shirts, and a diamond ring—in addition to his four cars: a 450 SEL Mercedes Benz, a 633 CS1 BMW, a Cadillac Seville, and a Volkswagen Rabbit. He also owns two three-story brownstones and is, in the words of the teenagers, "coming off strong." Darryl has been a dealer in heroin and cocaine for ten years. When he was nine years old he already controlled a crew of kids who sold joints at school. Today, at nineteen, he is a veteran.

> I first started out selling joints as a kid. This was my first real crack as a businessman. About a year or so after that I was a runner for dudes like Movie Star and Bobby W. I was so young then I didn't know exactly what I was running [selling], but I had an idea. My older brother and me both had

good reps in the street. I think it was Spencer, who was a numbers banker, who put the word out about us. And that's how I came into the coke business. I was too young to sniff it. And they spoke on [banned] heroin, so all I could do was smoke a little reefer and I didn't even like it that much. I was in a position where I could be trusted.

Darryl has made more than $500,000 in a single year from the sale of drugs. He is among the elite in an economic structure where the highest achievers are the most vulnerable and few stay on top for very long. It's a chancy business.

I had a couple of setbacks, the usual ripoffs from street scum, you know. I've had motherfuckers come in my place in broad daylight and take coke out of my crib [apartment]. Shit like that. But I was a kid. I didn't know no better. I had to learn the hard way. I had to cop me some protection and set up my operation, my organization, so nobody could touch it. I learned early don't trust yo' momma when it comes to money. After I took them busts, you know, I couldn't get no drugs at all. The fact that I was young and that the scum that took the shit was later found and shot and some of the shit was recovered— that was the only reason I'm alive today. The nigger did not want to hear that I lost the shit. Or somebody stole the shit. Or it accidentally fell in the tub. You know—fuck that—that's just yo' ass. After this shit happened, I still couldn't get no drugs unless I bought them. I scraped around and got two grand. I ain't had to borrow a dime since then. And that was damn near seven years ago.

In 1977 I started to get all my drugs on consignment. Not that I had to but because my coke connection, who was Cuban, considered me part of his clique. At that time, I couldn't speak Cuban but I could understand some of it. But now I can speak [Spanish] fluently. At first I would get one eighth [four ounces] of a key [kilo] and I was paying $7,000 and change for it then. His shit was the best around. I would put a one on it [cut it] and distribute the rest to my brother and his friends to sell. I thought it was a sign of manhood to have the money for coke up front but every time I did that he would look at me funny but he would take the money. Then one day I heard him say in Spanish, "No tiene cojones." I understood that to mean I wasn't a man because I wouldn't accept the coke without paying for it. I didn't understand until then that only those who couldn't be trusted according to his code would bring money to cop. I don't mean everybody. I mean those he had gotten to know over the years. And my not bringing money established a bond of friendship that was more lasting.

Darryl doesn't feel guilty about his activities. He sees selling heroin not as destructive to the community but as necessary to it because it provides money and jobs. Or (a more frequently voiced justification), "If I don't sell it, someone else will, so why not?" Besides, Harlem has changed since the 1960s, when heroin tore the community apart. Most heroin sales are to outsiders who come in to Harlem to cop (buy drugs). As Darryl says:

When I grew up in the '60s "heron" was a bad, bad drug only the scum of the earth indulges in. Cocaine dealers were the princes of drug dealers. But today heroin is the drug to sell because you can come off with so much cash. There is a higher rate of addicts out there so the kids are making money. Because there is a mix or variety of races coming up to cop like the Chinese, Puerto Ricans, Cubans, West Indians. This is because the best quality is in Harlem, so they come in and buy heroin and then they leave. Then also you have the Jersey crowd coming in, and all these add up. The purchasers are young and old. In the '60s the older Chinese were coming in on a regular basis to cop but now it's the younger Chinese brothers and sisters. They come up in a car, they cop, and they leave.

For inner-city youth, the temptation to test their skills in drug dealing is an attractive alternative to no job at all. Before long they begin to feel exploited by the higher-level dealers, and some, like Darryl, decide to start their own operations. But there's a kicker. The level of violence associated with heroin trafficking is gangland in style and execution. It is serious business. This is part of the ethos that separates teenagers like Darryl from their counterparts in Cleveland, Louisville, and elsewhere. Even in Harlem the heroin traffic is too rough for some.

A lot of the older brothers who deal in Harlem are backing off now, 'cause it's too much risk. Whereas the younger brothers are what we call fearless. You know they don't care about nothing; they sell it to anybody. So long as they get the money, they'll sell it. Regardless of who you are, they're not worried about nothing.

Darryl doesn't hang out at the candy store, where members of his crew of runners play pinball or shoot pool. Sometimes he stops by to rap with Mac, the owner, and some of the kids, but he goes there mainly to check on the crew's daily receipts. His social life takes place in an entirely different world, one filled with older women and men. His woman is a former wife of one of Harlem's major drug dealers; she is several years older than Darryl. They are part of a clique of big dealers and young hustlers on the make who spend their leisure time at exclusive discos and private after-hours clubs.

The potential of teenagers like Darryl will never be tested in the legitimate work world. Darryl has already achieved everything he aimed for. His success at street hustling has gained him status, prestige, money, and the possibility of becoming a folk hero. He is a winner on his own terms. (Or was. See the epilog for a note on Darryl's present situation.)

There are no winners on the streets of Greenpoint, Brooklyn, only losers. The young people in this working-class community spend much of their time in the old city park with its ornate, graffiti-smeared bandstands and broken benches. On a typical Saturday morning the park attracts a cross section of the community's residents. The youths, mostly boys in their middle and late teens and a few brave girls of the same age who drift in and out, combine to form a group of about twenty-five. All are white, as are the young mothers with their children who use the swings in another part of the park. Old men wait and watch along the iron fence that separates the park from the small area of stores and quiet bars across the street.

Today one of the boys, Biker, meets field study director William DeFazio in back of the bathrooms. "Billy, did you hear that Bones is dead?" he asks. "He got killed in McLarren Park last night. A spick killed him. Him, Jogger, Tall Johnny, Dirty John, Mush, and myself were in the park to mug Polacks."

Biker is Polish himself. By "Polacks" he means recent immigrants from Poland. These men work hard all week and tend to get drunk on the weekend. They are easy targets because they often carry all the money they have made in the past week. Jogger says he started mugging Polacks at fourteen. Every one of the boys has done it whenever he needed money.

"Two spicks came," Biker continues. "We got into words about cigarettes. We should have known if the Ricans were going up on all of us they must have been packing [carrying guns]. The spick pulled a gun, fired a shot over our heads. We all scattered. I heard another shot and Bones was dead. The spicks were gone. We called the cops. The ambulance came. Bones was dead.

"He laid in the park until this morning. Somebody went and got Tina. She cried over the body. We were all in the park until this morning. We were all pissed at the cops. M. said they should have a parade in Greenpoint because Bones was dead. He said the neighborhood was better off without that Guinea sonofabitch. F. came to see if Bones was really dead. He came and just smiled and walked away."

The cops hated Bones. He was the best thief in the neighborhood and an all-around troublemaker. All of the boys in the neighborhood are very upset about Bones's death—many of them are afraid that what happened to Bones will happen to them.

Most of the Greenpoint boys are school dropouts. Work for them is scarce. As in many other manufacturing villages within New York City, many small factories remain in Greenpoint. But they are more likely to hire recent adult immigrants from eastern Europe and Latin America than teenagers even for part-time jobs. Some of the boys find summer jobs and part-time work in the local factories and businesses, but there is a severe shortage of work for them. In consequence, many turn to theft. The majority spend their free time drinking in the park and getting high on pot or downers.

There are a few girls among the Greenpoint street kids. Many of them are trying to be as tough as the boys and project a "dykey" image. The boys tolerate their presence but do not form steady relationships with them. For the most part, the girls are excluded from the peer group.

DeFazio has lived much of his life in this economically depressed community. During the year that he served as a field study director he followed the lives of some fifty working-class boys like the ones in the park. He gave particular attention to one tightly knit peer group of about twelve boys. One day he invited several of the boys to his apartment for a rap session. Soon afterward his home was broken into and ransacked for anything of possible resale value. Today he sees one of the culprits, Buster, on the street outside the park with Biker and Jogger. Buster is making a phone call. His face is swollen and cut and his voice is terribly slurred. When he sees DeFazio he ends his conversation and hangs up the phone.

"Hi, Bill. Are you going to hit me? Don't hit me."

"I'm not going to hit you, Buster. I've had you arrested, that's enough for me."

"I'll try to get you your stuff back," Buster whines. "I'm sorry. I didn't even go into your house. They were just giving me stuff to watch. I didn't take anything."

"C'mon, Buster, they caught you with my television and some of my kid's jewelry and void bus tickets that had been used." (That was how the cops knew he had robbed DeFazio's house: his name was on the empty bus ticket books.)

The other kids start to laugh and make fun of Buster. "You asshole, you don't even know what void means. Buster, what does void mean?"

DeFazio asks, "How did your face get all bashed in? They did that to you in jail?"

Buster laughs sheepishly. "Nah, I fell down the subway steps. It's the ludes."

Jogger explains: "He's always falling down subway steps. That's why we're with him now. We picked him up and are trying to help him home. He always gets drunk and luded up and falls everywhere. He's always falling down subway steps."

"It's the ludes," Buster agrees. "When they robbed your house it was the ludes. If we didn't do the ludes we wouldn't have robbed your house. Billy, I never went into your house, I swear. You won't hit me, will you? I'll get your stuff back."

The robberies in the neighborhood have been occurring daily. The boys have hit Andy's Candy, Kim's Florist, Busy Bee Supermarket, Sherman's appliance store, jewelry stores on Manhattan Avenue, and St. Cecilia's Church. When they robbed St. Cecilia's of two solid-gold crucifixes they realized that it would be impossible to fence them or melt them down, so they dumped them in garbage cans in Monsignor McGoldrick Park.

The Greenpoint boys rob not only for the money but also for the excitement. Going geesing (stealing) is a social event. In this way the boys demonstrate their competence in a world that for the most part is hostile to them and seems to offer them no future. "Do you want to know why we rob?" Jogger says to DeFazio. "We rob because there's no work for us. If we can find work we wouldn't rob."

Often the boys try to involve DeFazio in their robbing. Today one of them, Red, approaches him in the park and tries to sell him a gold necklace.

"Forty dollars, Billy, just $40. It's worth at least $120. It's solid gold."

"What happened to your job?"

"I got fired."

"From the pizza place?"

"No. I quit the pizza place, it was too much. I got fired from Key Food."

"When did you start stealing? Is this necklace the first thing you stole?"

"I stole a bike, ten speed; I got $20 for it. I stole it the day I got fired. I got to live. Then I stole the necklace. C'mon, Billy, you can afford it. Give me $35 and it's yours. C'mon, give it to your girlfriend."

For every Darryl Conway there are a thousand Greenpoint boys. These young men are deeply pessimistic—"How do we know that we're not living in hell right now?" Jogger asks. Many of them have given up on the notion of the good life and are settling into lives of drugs, alcohol, and thieving. Why should they go to school when there aren't any jobs for those who graduate from high school or college? Why go to college when the few jobs that are available don't require a college education?

Two of the Greenpoint boys, Biker and Jogger, are continually working at jobs at which they are expected to learn while they work. But the learning is slow and they often "fuck up," as they put it, before becoming qualified for better-paying work. When they can't find work, they steal.

In another generation the Greenpoint boys would have been in much demand in the local factories. Their younger brothers would be involved in sports leagues; their sisters would find work in local stores or businesses in midtown Manhattan. But today the jobs are being fought over by adults and the young school dropouts are flirting with jail and death. Robbery and homicide rates have reached record levels among youth in U.S. cities. In one year of field research with the Greenpoint boys, DeFazio documented enough robbery and vandalism to more than adequately subsidize constructive work for each of the boys.

"We've all been busted," Biker says. "I've been busted for breaking and entering and stealing. I was going to steal a safe. We scooped everything out. They brought us to the precinct when they caught us and asked me a couple of questions. My old man beat me up. He beats me up whenever I get into trouble."

"Biker's right," says Jogger. "We all steal. Most of the time. Every day. I was unemployed for a while and my mom was taking care of me. I worked two jobs and when I don't work I steal. Like I'd steal meat."

Meat?

"You'd buy meat if I brang you meat, put it that way. Anybody would buy meat. They don't give a shit. You knock on someone's door and with inflation and all they jump at the offer. The first apartment you go to and they take it all."

Jogger's comments are typical of the explanations offered by the Greenpoint boys for stealing. The most frequently cited rationale is need for money; in fact, many of the kids say that crime is not justified when there is no need. A small proportion of the youth in the communities we studied commit crimes such as shoplifting, car theft, and drug dealing for other reasons: to relieve boredom, to impress peers, because they are drunk or stoned, or to gain revenge. But for the most part the teenagers who steal do so because they want some material thing (clothes, drugs, car parts) that they cannot acquire in any other way.

The Greenpoint boys are involved in an extremely self-destructive version of adolescent street life. Buster epitomizes this "Greenpoint youth syndrome." Not long ago DeFazio ran into him on the GG train to Queens. He was stuttering again, stoned on Quaaludes.

"I'm going to my drug program, I'm clean," he whined.

"You're clean? Buster, you are stoned, anybody can see that you're stoned."

"It's just beer."

"Don't bullshit me, Buster. Who robbed the jewelry store? You robbed the jewelry store, didn't you?"

"I didn't know what got into me, it was the ludes."

"You robbed the store all luded up, and with the precinct around the corner. You are just dumb, Buster."

"I thought I could do it. I smashed the window and started to grab the jewelry in the window but I couldn't grab it fast enough and I couldn't run when they grabbed me. It was the ludes."

"Buster, how many times have you been busted since you robbed my house?"

"Four or five times. I can't remember."

Buster is not the most competent of thieves. He is almost always stoned on ludes and beer. He is continually getting caught robbing and is in and out of drug treatment centers. Some of his robberies could have been designed by Mack Sennett. Once he and another boy robbed a jewelry store. They smashed the window with a brick and the window fell on them, knocking both of them out. The store owner called the cops and an ambulance.

It does not take extensive clinical training to see that Buster is sending out a call for help. He desperately wants to be stopped before he kills himself, but the people in the community who might help him are already overburdened by their existing caseloads. They lack the resources to reach out to the Greenpoint boys and help them out of their hell. Some of the boys eventually get out on their own; some, like Bones, never make it. Even for those who do escape, there seems to be no choice but to spend their adolescent years on the streets.

The street is the ultimate equal-opportunity employer. There are no working papers or application forms to fill out: no time clocks, bosses, or dress codes. But the occupational hazards are many. Among them are prison, drug addiction, depression, and death. Why do teenagers enter this risky and often unrewarding occupation?

It is evident that for many kids in low-income communities hustling is just that: an occupation. Darryl refers to himself as a businessman. Hustling is work, not play. It is not particularly healthy or safe, certainly not recreational. Even those who deal in cocaine or heroin—the drugs of choice for large numbers of customers—view these drugs as something to make money from, not as something to enjoy.

Many of the kids in the street economy begin as consumers: buyers of "nickel" and "dime" (five- and ten-dollar) bags of marijuana, "tens" of cocaine, joints of angel dust. Consumers easily become dealers—especially in the case of marijuana—because they can buy in quantity and set up their own operations. And if they happen to live in Harlem, they have the community's ethos of survival to draw upon.

In Harlem, hustling often means surviving. It is a way of life for many residents, and those without other means of support are drawn to it. It is part of the rhythm of the community—it is expressed in the music blasting from radios, windows, and shops; in the proud strut of the true Harlemite; in the gaity of street corner raps; and in the parked luxury cars. In Harlem the number halls are visible and busy, operating with little attempt at concealment. The many bars, after-hours clubs, and liquor stores are familiar haunts of number runners, prostitutes, and drug dealers. And Harlem is the capital of the drug world.

Harlem has been the Mecca of drug dealing since the 1950s. While many of the other ethnic neighborhoods in New York have specialized in other markets—pornography, clothing, jewelry, food—within the city's vast illegal economy, Harlem continues to be a center for underground transactions primarily because of ecological factors. It emerged as a market for legal and illegal vice before it became a black community in the 1920s and 1930s. Today, although the famous nightclubs, theaters, restaurants, and other entertainment spots have for the most part vanished, a lively market for drugs, sex, and gambling thrives unabated. The key to the success of this illegal economy is Harlem's accessibility to more affluent white and black patrons.

The increased involvement of youth in the drug market dates from the 1960s, when New York State passed the Rockefeller "get tough" law. This legislation carried heavy criminal penalties for adult heroin and cocaine dealers. As a result, many juveniles were recruited into the lower reaches of the drug market so that if they were arrested they could escape the mandatory penalties to which adults are subject.

This is not to say that kids who grow up in the hustling environment are inevitably drawn into the life of the streets, or even that once they enter it they can never leave. But entry into the straight world becomes more difficult as time goes by, especially if hustling turns out to be highly rewarding, as it does for a fortunate few.

In every economic system there are some who are at higher levels than others. The underground economy is no different. In a pyramid-type diagram one would see the majority of teenager hustlers at the bottom and a small elite at the top. Darryl is among the elite. He was selected by older hustlers into an opportunity structure that elevated him to a position that few teenagers can attain and even fewer are capable of sustaining and succeeding in. As a runner—the entry-level job—Darryl was able to establish himself in the drug-dealing underworld. Native intelligence did the rest.

> One of the ways I got into the money end of things is that I started thinking for myself. And there were a couple of other factors you might say that helped me do what I had to do. The first thing was to not be loyal to one dude. Now let me explain that. It used to be that if you had a connect and he was giving you good stuff and you was making plenty of money, there was no need to find another connect. But things changed over the last few years because I could see, and lots of others could see, that the connect was in control. So instead of having one connect who controlled you, you would have several connects and not be loyal to any single one of them.
>
> Another thing you got to understand is that the connect would string you along for years with him making the bulk of the cash. He would never let you accumulate enough money to buy big enough to start on your own. And he damn sure wasn't going to let you meet his connect. So he had you under his control. What I did was establish several connects until I got $10,000. Then I bought my own dope. I usually offed [sold] about three hundred quarters [$25 packages] a day.

Selection by an established drug dealer is an important part of the process by which one enters the drug market. It's a sort of apprenticeship in which one learns by doing. Darryl explains:

> The breaks are made mostly through an older brother. Say I got this younger brother doing something for me and he's doing well. He's like doing five or six hundred joints a day. Instead of me going to do something uptown with some other people, I'll just give it to him, and he might give it to some other brothers that he is with. But nobody knows that he is giving it to me. Now he's getting the money, he's leading. You figure that one young brother may know ten and the connection is made. Whereas I'm controlling it through one, it's moving on.

Darryl adds these comments on the differences between success and failure:

> The kids are much smarter today than I was back then. I would say an addict was a loser but then I would be curious to try the shit [heroin]. Whereas the kids today will say well, he is a loser and that's that. And any other heavy drugs are just for making money because they have been warned by the older brothers and sisters. The ones which are doing exceptionally well are ones that finished school. But most of them don't know how to take that money and do something with it. There are a few exceptions. The more they make, the more they may put aside and that keeps the money coming.

What about the ones who don't make it?

> A lot of the younger brothers in the street today are not at school. They are just roaming the streets and that opportunity don't come at you unless you are in certain cliques and since they're just roaming the streets, they build up a lot of animosity. They might not like this fellow here because he's making money and may have the females he likes and the BMW or the Mercedes. So they'll smoke dust and get high and instead of holding it inside of them, the dust brings it out—but in the wrong way. Whereas they might not approach the fellow who they are against, they'll approach anybody who is there, and that could lead to stabbing and shooting, or they hurt themselves. By them not going to school it confines them and their minds are very small and so they turn to violence. They never really take it out on the person who's actually the cause, which really isn't the cause anyhow.

Darryl has kids like C.C. and Zero in mind, but he could be talking about the Greenpoint boys as well.

For the losers of the street world, violence becomes a way of life. As Darryl says,

> When you find a group of kids together in the streets, they usually have pistols and it's nothing to get a pistol. Even now, when they have that new law in New York about pistols, it don't mean nothing. 'Cause I see more pistols now than I did before, and that's because the streets are getting tougher. In order to protect yourself, you get into artillery. Like I said, when a stranger walks in they know that they're a stranger and they want to protect themself. And then again, they also have gangster complexes. You know everybody wants to be bad, so this is more or less the custom, which has been passed on. They don't just carry them guns, they use them.

In the 1980s teenagers in the nation's cities are getting into crime in a big way. Young people are increasingly entering the major felony categories: burglary, murder, bank robbery, drug dealing, rape. Many of today's kids have given in to an overwhelming sense of desperation and despair. Young teenagers in the inner cities place little value on life. As a result, the risks they take in the pursuit of recognition and material possessions mean little to them. Most street teenagers are ambitious, though. They have a street kind of ambition—a street work ethic that translates into the slogan "I've got to get mine." They are highly motivated to do something for themselves and for their families, be it legitimate or illegitimate. And the illegal economy is so vast and the profits are so lucrative that kids find it hard to resist the temptation to become involved, especially when they are chosen by elite hustlers.

It is clear, however, that few young people in the underground economy are capable of making a living solely from their hustling activities. Most of them do not have a definite role or occupation in the hustling world, which means that they engage in whatever income-generating activity comes along. A young person who is desperate for money is just as likely to carry groceries or wash windows as steer a drug sale. But when teenagers find a hustle that pays off, they tend to stay with it.

This very human quality—which is nothing more than the time-honored drive to "get ahead"—explains why the underground economy tends to flourish in direct proportion to decreases in regular employment opportunities and public spending for education, employment, and training. This is especially true of the more exploitive illegal drug market. As a result, in the most impoverished communities the greatest business growth tends to occur in the illegal sectors of the underground economy.

We do not believe that young people in the underground economy have some sort of predisposition toward unconventional behavior. Their acts are the products of the options available to them; the street is the last resort. As Darryl puts it, "Whatever goal you shoot for and miss, you know you can always come back out here on the streets and survive."

5
Players and Ho's

I don't exactly fill out a W2 form after I turn a trick.
—Margo Sharp

ooksey's, D's Inferno, Club 437, McDonald's, and the mall are familiar hangouts for teenagers in Louisville. The mall is located in downtown Louisville; although it is integrated, it is a meeting place for black youth from all over the city. Many of the teenagers hustle in the pool rooms and discos, peddling marijuana and sex.

For the young women, hustling is synonymous with prostitution. Indeed, in all the cities we studied, prostitution is the main occupation for girls in the underground economy—girls like Donna White, who hustles in Louisville's mall area.

> I am 19 years old. About two years ago my parents moved to a little town called Madisonville, Kentucky. I hated that place. But I stayed long enough to finish school at Norman Hopkins [High School]. I wanted to go places and see different things and not stay in that damn place. I wanted to make something out of myself so I left and came here to Louisville. I couldn't find no job for nine months here so I met up with some friends who told me I could hustle and make some money. They said they would show me how. All I had to do was learn.
>
> So I first started hustling in the pool rooms and pushing a few petty drugs. My boyfried and/or his friend would stand in the pool room or out in the hall and wait till they saw some men, soldiers, businessmen, or whatever, and ask them if they wanted to have some sex. If they said yes, he would steer them over to the pool room and then tell me where to go meet them.

In the Hough district of Cleveland, dilapidated, burned-out structures from the 1960s riots are still visible. The housing consists mainly of single-family units. It is odd to see so many old houses, many in the grand style, decaying, unpainted, and broken. Hough is the ghetto of Cleveland. Its citizens, black and white alike, seem helpless to change it. The community is bankrupt economically, politically, and socially. Many feel that Hough is being punished for the "sins" it committed in the 1960s.

Pearl Varnedoe has worked as a prostitute in the Hough area and downtown near the University of Cleveland since she was fourteen. Pearl left home in order to "make money and live free." She says hustling came easily to her because "my parents had a club that always had pimps, whores, and gamblers in it."

> My mother was always beating me. My father tried to make her stop but he couldn't. My mother was always drunk and she couldn't stop that either. My father ran this after-hours club and when I left home I met up with some of them from his joint and they turned me out [set me up as a prostitute]. I always had real big titties and a nice body. As a matter of fact, the vice squad know me on sight and arrest me sometimes just to have something to do. I've been arrested about 21 times. They never knew I was a minor during all the time I spent there. When I went home to check on my father, I found out my mother had been beating my brothers and sisters too. Our neighbor had called in a child-abuse worker to talk to her, she told me she knew about my being on the street and filed a delinquency report with the juvenile authorities.

In Meridian, Mississippi, a large naval base on the outskirts of town has created a thriving market for drugs and sex. Thus the young people in Meridian perceive numerous opportunities in the illegal economy. The young men between the ages of 16 and 20 are the players or pimps, and the young women between the ages of 13 and 20 are the prostitutes—making prostitution the main source of illegal income for youths. Teenagers like Curly and his girls make up the "supply side" of prostitution in Meridian.

Curly is eighteen years old. His hustle is young women. He's a "player" and they are "ho's" or "tricks." (In Meridian "trick" refers to the prostitute or seller of sex; in New York the converse is true—"trick" refers to the buyer of sex.)

> I have one or two girls on the street. I still got a couple of them doing things for me. You know I gotta have that paper [money]. The only rule I have is that my main lady don't go out there. The others I have them boosting, tricking, whatever, as long as they keep giving up the money. See, baby, you do what you have to do to survive in this world now. The more money they have, the more I have. They do what they want to to get it. And when I ask them for it, I get it. Sometimes I'll help out if I get hip to someone who wants to make a buy. I'll let them know. But it depends on how much they get and how much I need. But I don't take all of their money. I usually leave them a little. And I don't feel I'm responsible for putting no ho on the street. Look, they are out there trying to be grown. They put themselves out there. If I didn't take their money, they would give it to someone else. Them tricks ain't gonna be nothing but whores. All I did was fuck them a couple of times and they started giving me money. See, a woman doesn't have to sell her body for a man to pimp her. There are plenty of women that are smart and pretty with good jobs and taking care of men. That's pimping.

Among Curly's "tricks" are Maylee Jones, Clara Thompson, and Dorothea Caddy, aged sixteen, sixteen, and seventeen, respectively. Here's what they have to say about "the life":

Maylee: There ain't no jobs around here. Besides I can make more money doing this. Sometimes I make one hundred or two, sometimes more, sometimes less. If I had a job, I wouldn't make that much. If I could make as much money in a job as I do hustling, I would work. The Navy boys they spend a lot of money. All these old white men do too. Anyway around here they give all the good jobs to the white people.

The most important thing in my life right now is surviving. That's all I believe in. Well, I believe in God but not preachers 'cause all the preachers do is ride around in Cadillacs and wear silk suits.

Clara: I have four boyfriends who give me $15 a week to go to bed with them. I only go out with one of them. The money I get I just spend it on clothes and stuff to get high with. I don't like to do it too much. I think it might do something to me. All the men are young, in their 20s. I give them a bit here and there but they give me the money on time. I like to show my legs and breast. It fascinates me to watch men cream.

Dorothea: I started tricking because I didn't know what time it was. I was at a friend's house getting high and they said, hey, you want to turn a trick for someone? And I said, it depends on the cash, what time, and who. At that time, I needed the money, you know. My boyfriend was there and I didn't know he was no pimp. But he kept encouraging me to do it. Anyway, after that I set my own thing up with one of my girlfriends. I have them [johns] call her. I used to have them call my pimp till I got rid of him. He got mad, but he knew I could fight him if he tried some shit like hitting on me. I didn't need him anymore, you know. I only had him for protection and the first time I went to jail for fighting, the man was out of town. I would make $150 or so and put $75 back and show him the rest, and he would give me $25 of that plus what I had, you know. He didn't know what time it was.

Dorothea dropped out of school in the ninth grade. At seventeen she organized a group of teenage prostitutes and set up a brothel in a fashionable black section of town.

Young women in each of these cities—and in New York as well—are shocked and depressed by the bleakness of their situation. Many do not believe they have a choice between getting a job and hustling. Hustling—meaning prostitution—is the only choice. (Theft and prostitution are often combined, but prostitution is by far the easiest, most convenient, and most profitable form of illegal activity for these teenagers.)

Most girls are recruited into prostitution, but some are tricked, coerced, or charmed into the life. The latter are talked into believing that it is an exciting life complete with fine cars and endless amounts of money. There is a note of self-delusion in some of their comments, like "A lot of the men are lonely and I feel I can help them" or "Most of the time the tricks don't know what time it is, so you can get their money."

While there are adult role models and community institutions that try to steer teenagers away from the life, many find the incentives too strong. Margo Sharp's life as a prostitute in Harlem illustrates the careers young women pursue in the underground economy.

Margo's parents separated when she was four years old. Her mother re-married, and during the ensuing years her father made sporadic appearances. When Margo was twelve or thirteen her mother became embroiled in domestic problems with her stepfather. Arguments and fights were common. Margo's mother began to have relationships with other men, including some of her husband's friends. One of those men had a traumatic impact on Margo.

My mother had an affair with this man who was later to become my step-father. Well, he had this friend, best friend no less, who was this little horny Dominican motherfucker. I was 12 years old then and I knew about sex and all of that, although I had never had sex. He would come around the house all the time and even though my mother was seeing my stepfather, this guy would come over sometimes and they would laugh and drink and my step-father would leave them alone sometimes because he trusted his friend so much. Well, my mother and this little Dominican started to have a thing be-hind my stepfather's back. And this little motherfucker was so horny, he wound up fucking my mother's best friend too.

Anyhow, one day I was upstairs doing my homework and he comes into my room and tells me he wants to talk to me. I don't remember if anybody was home or not that day, but I assumed he was gonna talk about my mother and their little thing, you know. So he told me to sit on the bed next to him. And I did. Still not thinking anything about it. Well the next thing I know he's taking my blouse off. And all the time he's asking me if I feel anything. Well I don't know why I didn't scream or anything but I just sat there. After he had taken off my panties, the only thought I had in my mind was not to panic. Not to scream because I had read all about how men had killed women and kids molesting them or something, and I wasn't about to say a thing. So he took off my panties and the only thing that stood out in my mind was how big he was. It seemed like he was as big as a tree trunk, I swear to God, I was hurting so bad, I was so sore. I felt, my God, what did he do to me? Well, when it was over, he helped me put back on my clothes and I sat on the bed for a long time just thinking.

I never told my mother anything for two years. And when I did her reac-tion was typical of women in love. She slapped me. She thought I was lying for years after I told her this. She didn't believe nothing I told her. One day two years later this little bastard drove up to my house to see my mother. Well my mother told me to come out and say hello to him. But I was not too excited about seeing the little fucker ever again. So I refused. But she insisted so I went out to say hello. But when I saw his face I just got angry. The window of the car door was down. And he reached his face out to kiss me and I spat in it. My mother jerked me away and slapped me. But I grabbed her arm and told her I was no kid any more. I was 14 years old and that she had no reason to protect a man who had not only cheated on her by fucking her friend but had cheated on her by fucking her daughter. She didn't believe me. Like I said, she thought I was lying. She was so in love with this faggot that she didn't believe her own daughter. I hated him for that more than his act against me because it made my relationship with my mother a stormy one for years to come.

Margo was fourteen then. Her mother was unwilling to assume responsibility for her wayward daughter, so she sent Margo to a social worker at the Children's Aid Society. After a series of bad experiences in a variety of schools, Margo finally dropped out. Considered gifted by her teachers, she could not make herself sit still long enough to complete her studies. Instead, she was habitually absent. Her lateness and absenteeism eventually resulted in expulsion.

Margo's attitudes about men were formed early. She was more game than most men could handle. Standing tall and shapely with big eyes and a warm, inquisitive intelligence, she was no child and knew it. After leaving school, she refused to work but always seemed to have money. Her mother occasionally asked her how she was able to get along without working, but Margo always had an explanation.

I would have $200, $300, $400 and my mother knew nothing about it. I wouldn't tell her where I had been. So half the time she didn't know. I didn't buy a lot of stuff or give her money because I was afraid she would ask me where I got it from. I tried to explain it to her one day. I told her a friend of hers, Mr. George, who was about 50 years old had hinted he wanted to have sex with me. So I jokingly told my mom that if he wanted it, it would cost him a hundred bucks. Well, she laughed and said, "Yeah, that's better than giving it to him for free." So in a way, I guess, she didn't really object to what I was doing.

By the time Margo was fifteen she was involved in casual prostitution, averaging two hundred dollars per customer. She was in the life as an "outlaw," that is, without benefit of a pimp. Her method was a bit unorthodox. When a man approached her, she would take the money from the transaction and give it to one of her male friends.

Sometimes my friend would look at me funny when I told him to hold the cash. It would be a few hundred dollars. And that I would be back later. I would go to a hotel and after it was over I'd go back to pick up my money. If a guy approached me and said I was beautiful and asked how much would it cost him to have me, I would tell him whatever came to my mind. If he looked well dressed and clean I would say $200, $300, $400. It depended on my mood. If I was real horny, I would react quicker but that didn't mean the price went down. I would just choose someone who I thought was good looking. Someone who I thought would be pleasant to fuck. Sometimes I would get off with these guys but most of the time I would pretend.

At least some liked it enough to pay high prices for it. It started out with offers of $100 or more for an hour or two. When they first started asking me I would decline, and then decided to stop being such a fool. I started accepting, not only money, but gifts, trips, etc. It was sort of like getting your cake and eating it too. I was not only compensated for time, but I was spent time with as well. The sexual acts were sexual acts. But if they brought on a smile, a kiss or hug the morning after, it was worthwhile. I felt not only wanted but needed. At the same time, a lot of lonely hearts were warmed. Call it what you will, I see my actions in a benevolent light. I enjoyed the money, spending highly, indulging in things I wouldn't normally have. The gifts were sweet. They showed a touch more of consideration. The men were usually much older than myself. I, in some cases, portrayed a prized china doll that they flaunted.

Yes, I did get tired of the life at times, but it was an experience, and I learned a lot. I met some very interesting people. I always tried to establish a good rapport with my friends. One never knows who one may need some day. But only as friends. My intimate relationships were always kept separate and never came about from a trick night. It was difficult at times having both a main man and my pastime, but I managed. In some cases, where I felt the person I was dealing with was due more respect, I would cool off my friendly encounters and devote myself to that one person.

For young women like Margo, prostitution becomes a distinctive lifestyle, known as "the life." But for the pimps or players, hustling sex isn't very different from any other kind of hustle. The young man usually has tried a variety of ways of earning money, finally settling on pimping as involving the least effort for the greatest reward. Ray-Ray Southern is typical.

I came to Meridian when I was 11 years old. I went to Oakland Heights Elementary School in the fifth grade. I got along very well with the teachers. We caught the city bus every day to school. I got out of school one day by playing sick and stole a bicycle. I had to go by the babysitter's house to pick up my little sister and brother. They were very happy to see me. My momma came home by the babysitter's house and found out about the bicycle. She asked me where it was and I told her somewhere else, but I didn't know where. Momma took me home and whipped me. The police came and talked to me and we got over that.

About three weeks later our house caught on fire. My sister was smoking a cigarette and threw the butt on the floor. After the fire, we changed schools and I met the wrong type of friends. I had a fight the first day of school. Later on, I stole another bicycle and I didn't get caught. I began to turn out with this girl I was running with. We would do things like stealing, smoking, drinking, and breaking out people's windows.

Everything was happening to me then. My girlfiend and I got caught in the act of love making. My mother was very upset. She wanted to whip me but my dad talked her out of it. She was upset because she didn't know I knew too much about sex. My mother talked to us about it but I wasn't listening. I liked what I was doing. After a few more incidents, we broke up because of her mother. So I met another girl. I was going over there every day. I was going to school but I would play hooky with her. We didn't stay together because all she wanted was sex. The first day of the next term I was kissing this girl and they said I had to go. This happened too many times. So I left because there was too many rules anyhow. You couldn't hold hands, you couldn't talk to white girls, etc.

I got into trouble again and this time they sent me to Columbia Training School. I was there for four months and two weeks. Three months later I was in more trouble—breaking and entering. I got some items out and sold them to the wrong person. I had to go back to the juvenile center. I was out one day and the next one I was in.

I got a job when I got out working at Morrison's [Restaurant] as a cook. But at $1.95 an hour, that's bullshit. At Morrison's they thought they had a real nigger working 'cause I really tried to keep that job. But that damn man [boss] was crazy. He started bitching with me. Now he knows a cook don't wash no damn dishes. I wouldn't do that shuffling routine, so I quit. I started stealing hams and making some money. I would take my girlfriend with me to the supermarket and I'd have a box underneath the cart. We'd walk around filling the box with steaks, pork chops, hams, chickens, all kinds of shit. I'd have tape in my pocket and some stamps with rope. This is so it would look like a package. That don't never fail to work. I'd steal about $1,500 worth of meat and sell it for $800. Sometimes I buy a little weed to sell. I pay $45 for an ounce or $150 for a pound and make more than $300 every three or four days. All I want is a Cadillac, two tons of weed, five pounds of crystal T, a nice house, and be financially well off. I would much rather work than hustle because working is steady. When you work you know where the money is coming from.

We did not find any consistent pattern in the backgrounds of young men who become pimps. Husbands, boyfriends, and transient players all play the role. Young boys sometimes identify with the player image—New York players set standards of dress and lifestyle that are widely imitated—but in most cases the motivation is economic necessity. Frances H., a close observer of the street scene in Meridian, described the situation of teenage pimps in this southern town as follows:

It's not that all these kids want to be players or hustlers. The first thing you think is they don't want to work. That's misleading. Most of them, and I mean the major portion of them, have tried at one time or another to get a job. They have beat down the doors of the unemployment offices. They have been in these stores, dealing with all these crackers who constantly make wisecracks and comments about how dumb they are and stuff like that. And they, rightly so, get tired of it. Then they come back out here on the street and say, "Fuck it. I'll make it any way I can. I'll be a player. I'll be a hustler. I'll be cool. I'll be clean." They want to have that paper. Just like everybody else does. You can't tell 'em they don't know what time it is because they think they do. So it ain't like they ain't tried. It's just that they got tired of all the bullshit. A lot of what this is about is discrimination. It's prejudice against these kids. Them young white boys can go to daddy and say, "I need a job" or "I need money" and get it. But these black kids have to kiss ass and then be told, "Ain't no jobs for you, nigger boy." So you know it ain't about not wanting to work.

The experiences of young people in other regions of the country reveal few differences in lifestyle and some basic similarities in values and outlook toward their immediate future. Most teenagers in the underground economy, regardless of region, maintain the traditional values of work, money, and success. Although these are limited commodities, the youths are as desperate in their search as anyone else.

One thing is clear—teenagers like Ray-Ray will more often than not find illegal opportunities more attractive than legal ones. Those who have had negative experiences in the work place, no matter how brief, will move on to the underground economy and try to forge an identity there. Ray-Ray, however, is the first to admit that he is not going to get rich stealing meat, selling marijuana, or even pimping.

Some teenage hustlers do manage to find jobs. But often they leave within a few months because the demands of the job appear to be too great, especially when hustling seems to offer an easier life. Here's what Margo has to say about her brief career in the nine-to-five world:

If you're the type that can never be without a job, not having one may cause a problem. I'm not that type. I can live with or without one. I've never been one to worry about work. Occasionally I might find myself in a jam, but I believe things work themselves out and they usually do. Not working doesn't bother me so much as having to do that regular nine to five. I hate straight hours, time clocks and suspicious bosses. I enjoy not having to deal with the same environment and people within that structure on a daily basis. That type of contact, being constant, tires me. I love to free-lance. I enjoy change in work situations. I'm trying other ways to make money, not necessarily legal ways, and I'm open to ideas.

Not working steadily, I will admit, causes problems for me. Because the cash flow isn't there all the time. Naturally I will find other ways to make up for this lack of money, but the market isn't always open to me. When I say this, I'm speaking of the people I may be with at that particular time in my life, or my access to the street. Making illegal money is a whole different scene. It's part of what I categorized before as free-lancing. Some examples of free-lancing would be anything from hocking your personal property or someone else's, to dealing drugs or selling yourself, borrowing, mediating, touting, you know. If you can do any of these and hold down a tax-paying job, you're alright. But if you can keep this life up and survive from it alone, you're doing better.

One thing about prostitution, it's a tax-free job. The risk is the thrill. I feel one has to be adventurous, daring, and mischievous to a point. The first thing one has to keep in mind is that you're going to get caught. Not by the authorities, no! That's the last thing in my mind. When I say get caught, I mean by the street. If you're dealing in anything against the law, you always have heavy competition. If your game is good, people want to tear it down. It's a constant battle in the streets for survival. There is a lot of planning, scheming, lying, cheating, and a little bit of fear out there. The fear has to be natural or you're doomed. You have to love danger.

I hate what society considers normal. So I find other ways of living within this world, without letting it bother me. If it bothers others, that's their problem. Every man for himself. When it comes to money you will find very few are going to help you make it. And if you're the type that helps others, you'll find yourself taken for a sucker. So you resign to helping yourself. The advantages of this street business, hustling, it's on you. You wake up, eat, sleep, you don't punch no clocks, you don't conform to no rules and regulations or courtesy to co-workers, customers, bosses, clients, patients, staff, etc. Best of all, you don't pay taxes either.

Margo's work history includes both legitimate and illegitimate roles. Although she possesses the skills to work in a mainstream occupation, she has not developed the discipline to remain in a job very long. This is partly a result of immaturity. However, it is a well-known fact that few teenagers maintain jobs for more than a few months at a time. It is Margo's street and family values that have kept her at odds with the straight world. Her forays into the regular workaday routine are always of short duration because there is more money to be made on the streets. There is always an available market of older men who will buy her services, yet she sees the weakness of her own game. She knows that a prostitute's life—even a high-class call girl's life—is a short one. She knows she won't always have a youthful face and body. And when things get tough—for instance, after a brutal trick—she looks for work in a regular job. Margo sees no discernible difference between her straight-out prostitution and what other women do as secretaries or as wives at home.

Margo's views are not shared by the parents and friends of most of the teenage prostitutes we met. There appears to be a double standard operating in this area: the pimps/players are seen as smooth, slick, and smart, the girls as stupid and dirty. Feelings of revulsion and pity were expressed by some of the parents, while others did not seem to know or care what their children were doing. Many of the girls turned to prostitution after becoming pregnant and being rejected by their boyfriends and parents.

Once a girl enters the life, ties with family and friends are usually broken. It is common practice for a pimp to insist that his girls sever all such relationships. Independent prostitutes like Margo may maintain contact with their friends but tend not to explain to them what they do for a living.

In addition to the availability of prostitution as an option and the perceived disadvantages of straight jobs, certain experiences during childhood and adolescence can lead to a career in prostitution. Rose M. of Hough is a case in point.

Things were okay at home until I turned 13. I moved out when I turned 13 and quit school. My stepfather and I couldn't get along any more. I kept moving in and out until I was 15. My mother didn't mind because I always let her know where I was and went by to see her when my stepfather was at work. I didn't have to worry about supporting myself then. When I was 14 I got put on probation for not going to school. At 15, when my mother died, my stepfather sent my sister and myself down south to stay with our real father. I didn't like my father so I came back to Cleveland to stay with a friend. I was getting a social security check from my father so I had money.

The girl I was staying with worked the streets. She was only 16. I didn't have to but I started working with her. It was scary but it was a living. I grew up very fast in the streets. I shot dope but I never got hooked. At 16 I got pregnant and left my man. I went to the Safe Space Station, a runaway shelter. The people were really nice. They tried to help, but I was used to being on my own. So I went back to my man and worked until I was seven months. I also shot dope while I was pregnant. The dope only made my baby small.

We moved from place to place after that. Then my stepfather had me put in D.H. and tried to take my baby. I stayed there for ten days, then went to a child-care center for three weeks. I turned 17 in there. The court placed me in the custody of the county. My social worker took me down and got me on welfare. Before that I was still turning tricks. I still worked some even though I was on welfare and got social security because I wasn't used to getting money once a month. I still moved from place to place. My son has never had a stable home until now, and he'll be two next month.

Now I'm 18 and I'm three months pregnant. One thing I promised myself, with this baby I'm not going to go through the things I went through with the first. I feel I have an advantage over most people my age and older because I know and have experienced things they'll never know. The only disadvantage is I don't have as much interest in men like I had. My pimp beat me up and tried to make me have an abortion. But I ran away from him because I was tired of the streets and let myself get pregnant on purpose. I know I wasn't forced to get into the life. Because I used to do it a lot with my girlfriends after school to get money to buy extra clothes. When my mother would ask me where I got the clothes from I would tell her I exchanged them with friends. After my mom died and I wasn't going to my stepfather's anymore, I lived with the rest of the girls at my pimp's stable.

For some teenage girls, incestuous relationships with their fathers and encounters with pimps at school may have started them on the road to prostitution. Kate Strolls is a seventeen-year-old dropout who moved away from home after a series of incidents with her father.

I dropped out of school in the ninth grade. At this point I have no interest in going back. I used to live in the Woodland Projects apartments. It was ugly as hell. It had all these empty houses, old buildings, and winos everywhere. I first hooked up with this pimp at school. I started turning tricks in the afternoon and bringing some of the money home to my mother. She took the money and never asked me where I got it from. She just told me not to get myself killed.

My father moved away after we, my sister and me, got together and told my mother that he had been having sex with both of us and then threatening to kill us if we told anybody. I feel okay about the whole thing but my sister turned real mean and won't talk to nobody. She has no friends and stays at home with my brother even though she is old enough to be on her own. I don't feel that way about men. I just don't develop feelings for them when I'm working. And I prefer to be with women anyhow.

I had this woman stop me one night down on Prospect and give me $100 to go with her. I was scared but, shit, I figured I could out-fight the broad if it got too crazy. She had this nice place to stay and all this nice furniture and a man. She turned me out that night.

For many young women, a crucial factor is the lifestyles of the adult women who are closest to them. This was the case for Margo. Her adult role models were her mother, her aunt, and a very close friend of her mother who was active in civil rights, all of whom were rebels and fought private battles at home or public battles against society. Unlike many of the other girls in our study, Margo had a relatively stable home and social environment. She had opportunities to travel, to attend school and do well. But the examples set by her family, her early experiences, and the complexities of her own personality led her to choose the fast life. There is no doubt that young women like Margo could lead successful lives in a professional career were it not for one or two incidents that shaped their life patterns. As she herself explains:

As a baby, not from what I recall, but only hearsay, I was alert, smart, too fast for my britches, and loved to party and drink. One might say that I haven't changed a bit. I was walking at the age of six months, but didn't let go of my bottle till around four years. I was a year old and one still couldn't tell whether I was a girl or a boy, since I still had not grown hair. There was no way to add ribbons, bows or clips to my scalp. So I spent my first year as a child with an undefined sexuality. At eight months my mom was fed up with me, so I say. She claims that it was in my best interest for her to have sent me to my grandparents in South America. This was for a period of three years. I've been told that as a toddler, I spoke too much, knew too much, ate too much, and never liked going to bed on time. I was spoiled, having been the first granddaughter, and yet was very charming and lovable.

At 3 1/2, I was sent back home to my mother, who by this time I'd forgotten. This, of course, was after having traveled throughout South America and the Virgin Islands. I wish they would have saved those trips now. I arrived at Kennedy International Airport via Avianca Airlines, escorted by my aunt, and was received by everyone from a to z that was a member of my family or knew someone in it.

My room was filled with an accumulation of toys over the past three years. Most of them I still have. One that I loved in particular was a teddy bear named Moy-Moy. He used to be white and fluffy, nowadays he is skinned of all his hair, dyed and ripped. One of the dolls I used to have was four feet tall. Now I was a tiny 3 1/2-year-old, so you can imagine in comparison to me this thing was a giant. Sometimes I honestly feel that parents are not practical. An example is that by the time I was five, my father, whom I rarely saw, had given me a collection of dolls from all different nations. By the time I was seven, the collection was destroyed. To this day, my mother still curses me out over it and calls me irresponsible.

I may sound ungrateful, but I'm really not. I really can't complain about my childhood. It's my teen years that I hated the most. I knew my real father as the man who came to give me money, or to take me shopping to buy things. He was very well off and he proved it to me. But I didn't want his fucking money. He deprived me of his presence. He deprived me of his love. What is money to try and replace that? I'll tell ya, it ain't shit. So I threw all of that in his face. I guess that's why he's been so reluctant to contact me now. He knows I hate what he did. All my life I've had negative feelings about my father due to the fact that in my eyes his time was too precious to spend with me. All these years I've denied ever having needed him, loved him, missed him, or wanting him. Now I wonder. I remember when I was real small. He would come in, pick me up, and put me on his shoulders. You see, my father was real tall and skinny and when he would lift me up, it seemed like—oh God—it was to the ceiling. It seemed so high to me. But I would hold my breath and close my eyes and in a few seconds I was on top of the world.

Teenage prostitutes, and the men who exploit them, have developed a negative self-image and considerable hostility toward members of the opposite sex. They are at risk of remaining in the criminal subculture as adults, and if they do not find better role models and opportunities that is the most likely prognosis. But these teenagers, street wise and cynical as they are, are not "lost" or "fallen," even though they may think of themselves in such terms. Timely intervention by caring adults could counteract the experiences that led them into prostitution and could guide them onto more constructive paths to maturity.

6
Crews

We felt that we were the hippest people and that the other people didn't know anything. When I was in the street with these people, we all had to live for one another. We had to live in a way that we would be respected by one another. We couldn't let our friends think anything terrible of us, and we didn't want to think anything bad about our friends.

—Claude Brown

In Harlem, high-rise public-housing projects are the most typical kinds of housing for young people and their families. Much has been written about the projects, most of it negative, like this description from James Baldwin's *Nobody Knows My Name:*

> The projects are hideous, of course, there being a law, apparently respected throughout the world, that popular housing shall be as cheerless as a prison. They are lumped all over Harlem, colorless, bleak, high, and revolting. The wide windows look out on Harlem's invincible and indescribable squalor: The Park Avenue railroad tracks . . . the unrehabilitated houses . . . the ominous schoolhouses . . . and the churches, churches, block upon block of churches . . .

The housing projects are a way of life for today's big-city youth. Many have never known any other home. In these high-density neighborhoods young people learn the prerequisites of survival early. Among them are the skills of self-defense and the importance of "running buddies."

When we say "early," we mean by the age of five or six. The following recollection shows why:

> I'll never forget the first day my mother sent me down alone. It was eleven floors to the lobby and then you were outside in the middle of the projects. I remember I was dressed in new clothes and had some kind of toy I was holding. I think I was five.
>
> It seemed like there were a million kids tearing around the courtyard. I had no brothers or sisters and I didn't see anybody I knew right away. Then

---

Manchild in The Promised Land (New York: Signet, 1965), pp. 270–271.

a slightly bigger kid came up to me and grabbed my toy. I wouldn't let go. He bashed me in the face. I dropped the toy and ran to the elevator. Blood was all over my new clothes. That was my introduction to the street. You never forget something like that.

This type of experience is a common tale of childhood in poor communities. To survive, one must learn to protect self and possessions, to fight for both self-defense and self-respect.

Throughout urban minority communities there is much emphasis among youth on the concept of respect. A positive legacy of the militancy of the 1960s and 1970s, this insistence on personal respect is also essential for survival. In the streets, where so many of the people one meets are strangers, a child learns quickly to avoid trouble where possible and to stand up to it when necessary. "You can have sixty fights and lose every one," say the kids who hang out in Harlem's Metro North housing projects. "The important thing is that you fought. You can't be a punk." This attitude is not simply a matter of personal pride. The child who is afraid to fight faces endless threats: money is extorted; bicycles are taken away; access to public facilities is denied. Under these conditions, parents naturally seek to protect their children, most often by keeping them home, calling them from work, and begging them to stay off the streets. But this is a losing proposition as the kids reach adolescence and turn to the peer group for protection and identity.

For youngsters in poor communities, the old cliché about safety in numbers takes on added significance. The need for peers or running buddies is evidenced in this brief excerpt from a youth's diary:

Today me, Tracy, Bernard and John were going up in the elevator to John's house. When we got to the eighth floor three boys from the Cigar Mob got on. One of them had a shotgun. He pointed it at Bernard. The other boys was laughing. They are younger than us. They go to junior high. I grabbed the end of the gun and pushed it away. We got to the twelfth floor and got off.

In some situations a peer group may develop into what youth call a crew, the contemporary descendant of the adolescent fighting gangs of the 1950s and 1960s. A crew is different from a peer group in that it has an explicit identity: a name, a pledge, a code of ethics, rules of behavior. One well-known crew, Zulu Nation, requires its members to wear beads. A member of another crew comments, "Those guys get upset if you don't have on your beads. I think some of those guys will break on [make fun of] you if you aren't wearing them."

There are running buddies and peer groups everywhere, and not just in low-income communities. The presence of crews, which have a more formal structure, generally hinges on the existence of a turf system in urban areas, as well as on positive support ("backup" or "back"), participation in informal sports competition, sharing of material resources, and the like. Crews differ from gangs primarily in their lack of emphasis on fighting for its own sake: although crews are quick to defend their members, they seldom go looking for fights and usually aren't organized for fighting. There is occasional inter-racial fighting, and there is always a turf of some sort to defend. But the chief goal of a crew, with few exceptions, is something other than fighting.

The root cause of the formation of a crew is a pressing need of some sort: for money, protection, recognition, success. For poor teens, all of these things are hard to come by. Even middle-class youths, who usually have access to at least some sources of recognition, occasionally feel drawn toward membership in crews.

Usually the chief need is for money. Adolescence is the stage of human development in which the individual moves away from the home, school-yard, and street corner. Adolescents begin to explore a much larger social and physical world than they could when they were in grade school. This explora-tion requires spending money. The hunger for cash grows throughout ado-lescence, and for poor youth, especially in the densely populated projects, there are few opportunities to earn it. Thus, if an opportunity to make money through collective activity comes along, a crew may be born.

Crews may be organized around illegal transactions or street crime— cocaine and marijuana dealers, purse snatchers, and shoplifters are organized into crews. But money is far from constituting the only basis for the organi-zation of crews. Crews may form along racial or ethnic lines or around spe-cific activities, such as sports, or forms of expression—a preferred style of music or dance (disco crews) or, in the case of the graffiti crews, art. (The va-riety of crew interests is illustrated by some of their names: Savage Wheels, Cocaine City Boys, Stone City Rockers, Midnight Rockers, Children of the Grave, 200 Public Animals, Bang Bang, Savage Lovers, Zulu Nation, Rolling Thunder Writers. Crews with names with "Rocker" at the end started as a result of the members' association with rock music and are in opposition to disco crews. Rocker also refers to break dancers.)

The graffiti crew epitomizes crew motivation, organization, and behavior. It can be either a self-contained crew or the "artistic subcrew" of a larger crew like Zulu Nation. It consists of seven to twelve young adolescents who take great risks to paint the name of the crew on subway cars and other public canvases in an attempt to reach as wide an audience as possible.

In a way, the graffiti subcrew is the PR department of the parent crew. Prestige, or "fame," is associated with reaching the widest possible public. Thus, a crew will attempt to be "king of number one," meaning the number 1 subway line, which runs up- and downtown on the West Side of Manhattan. There is less prestige associated with being, say, "king of number seven," which runs between Manhattan and Queens, or any other subway line with comparatively low ridership. Issac, a member of the graffiti crew known as Toy Crashing Artists, explains:

They know if they can throw it up [get their name on the side of a subway car] and maybe be king of the number one, or two or something like that—that's fame. Nobody want to be king of the LL because it don't make but three stops. Everybody will say, What line do you hit up [write on]? And if you say the number one, two, or something like that, it's okay but not the LL. It's prestigious to say I hit up on a popular train. The number one is the filthiest train. It's been pieced [written on] on every car.

The members of graffiti crews are for the most part quite talented and ambitious. Some are students at special high schools like the High School of Music and Art in Manhattan. Fourteen-year-old Issac has this to say about his "writing" activity:

I get along with my real father but he doesn't understand or like this writing that I do. I've explained it to him lots of times but he just doesn't like it. My stepfather didn't like it at first either, but one day I took him out to see a piece and he said, "Man, that's something; that's art." So he's more open to it. My moms of course really like what I do because she sees it all the time in my room. She's taken an interest now that I'm in school. But she told me I better not take any chances or get caught writing on the trains.

I'm Jewish, although I'm not really the religious type. I don't go around shouting about it. I'm the youngest one in my family. I have an older brother who's 17. I think he's in a crew too but he won't admit it.

I would like to be a commercial artist one day. I'm gonna be taking classes next year in visual arts. And I know commercial art is really where the money is so I'm gonna do that. I don't have any heroes or anything like that because I don't like sports and stuff. But my favorite painters are Michelangelo and Rembrandt.

Another crew member, Ali, also has an artistic career in mind.

My name is Ali and I live at 800 Riverside Drive. I live with my mother and step-father. My real father and I see each other a lot. He likes my writing and everything but he don't want me to get caught bombing [covering a large surface with spray paint] or anything. I don't do that anyway because I don't want to mess up and also because I do signs for people now and that makes me get better at writing. I didn't know as much as I do now until I met Issac here, he taught me a lot. Like how to shade and line. But now I'm as good as he is. I think it really is art, though, because piecing is three-dimensional, with colors and everything. And it's expressing your ideas, expressing how you feel. I want to do commercial art too. I want to do signs and things like that.

Most crew members are boys, although the larger crews have female members. There is a crew of female graffiti artists; in addition, a number of crews have been formed by girls who have developed a jumprope game ("double dutch") into a skillful combination of acrobatics and dance. Double-dutch crews sometimes engage in scheduled competitions with other crews, and two such crews, the Jazzy Jumpers and the Ebonettes, have appeared on television videos and were recently invited to perform at Brooklyn College.

The ages of crew members range from 8 to 30, but most members are in their mid-teens. The Cigar Mob is an exception. This crew is made up of about two hundred 8- to 12-year-olds who engage in a variety of petty hustles. The youth whose diary we quoted near the beginning of this chapter says of them:

> We know these little punks. They think they're real bad but we can handle them. It's when you're alone that they can be dangerous because there's a whole bunch of them. They collect guns and some of them are selling drugs and they're only 11 and 12 years old.
>
> This [incident] with the boys from the Cigar Mob was light. It did shock us though. We're in high school and we think we run those buildings. Now here's this whole gang of crazy little kids coming up and they are just nuts. They'd just as soon kill you and if you fight with one of 'em the rest will jump you too.

The activities of the Cigar Mob are more random than those of the typical crew, which often show signs of careful planning. A case in point is the Co-caine City (C.C.) Boys, a crew that "graduated" from petty hustles to semi-legitimate business activity. Individual members of the crew accumulated substantial amounts of cash through burglary, robbing of drug dealers, and the like. They then pooled their resources and used the money to establish a chain of small candy stores that, among other things, sell loose cigarettes and joints and provide pinball machines and other entertainment for their youth-ful customers.

The case of the C.C. Boys points up an important feature of crews: they mimic the structures of the larger society. The C.C. Boys run an organized business; graffiti and disco subcrews serve as advertising agencies for their crews. Some large crews, like Zulu Nation, have chapters in various parts of the city. Censor, a member of a rival crew, describes the Nation with more than a touch of envy:

> They are like the Mob, very organized and powerful. Because they have chapters. I don't know how many, but it's a lot. They have chapters in almost all the boroughs. They have the Chief Mob and the Gestapo in Long Island. They are black and Puerto Rican. They have a chapter on 125th Street [Manhattan]. They have Chilly Youth—mostly young kids like the Cigar Mob. They have Rock Steady, who promote break dances. They have the Soul Sonic Force too. And a lot of other crews get backup from Zulu Nation.

The Zulu Nation are the most organized and they make money by pro-
motions through Soul Sonic Force. They get money from Chilly Youth because they mug people. And they get money from these video game operations in the city. And the Zulu Nation buys guns with this money. Everybody
know the Zulus be strapped [carrying guns].

The comparison of the Nation to the Mob should not be taken too seriously. It's true that many crews engage in illegal activities, but they are far from
constituting a kind of Junior Mafia. The involvement of crews in the
underground economy is a reflection of the fact that the urban cash economy
has become the chief means of survival for millions of Americans of all classes
and backgrounds. A small proportion of poor teenagers are entrepreneurs in
the illegal sector of the cash economy. In large cities like New York, this proportion becomes a large absolute number. For them this activity is a business.

As noted earlier, many crews are organized to make money. One way in
which a crew becomes a money-making operation is through the efforts of a
strong leader. A leader with the necessary contacts and some degree of
charisma (like Darryl, the teenage heroin and cocaine dealer, or Afrika Bam-
baataa, the leader of Zulu Nation) can readily convert a group of kids with
few claims on their time into an organized crew. The crew may engage in
burglary, break dancing performances, shoplifting, car theft, drug dealing,
rapping, scratching (one of a number of techniques invented by Harlem disc
jockeys, involving use of both hands to spin a record backwards and for-
wards to evoke a scratching redundancy), extortion, or ownership of small
candy stores, pool rooms, and pinball rooms. Whatever the activity, the
salient feature of the crew is its advanced degree of organization.

Along with a formal structure come strict rules and a code of ethics. According to Censor,

> The loyalty to the crew is important. You can't belong to two rival crews at
> the same time. Slashing [destroying other crews' graffiti] is not allowed because
> you don't want trouble for your crew. Most of the time calling for a back is
> forbidden. And you don't go bombing [painting large surfaces] alone. Oh
> yeah, and in some crews you have to rack up [steal] in order to be a member.
> Different crews have different rules. My friend wanted to join MPC and he
> had to take a piece and go up to a man in the street and ask for a light. If the
> guy didn't have a light he had to pull the trigger. He went up to the guy and
> the guy didn't have a light and Jason kept asking the guy, "are you sure you
> don't have a light, check the other pocket," until the guy finally walked
> away. He pulled the gun but it was empty. He was so scared he didn't know
> what to do. But he got in.

The rules of a crew can develop into a complex system that shapes the activities of members. Graffiti artists, for example, make a firm distinction

between "tagging," or simply writing one's name on a wall, and "piecing," or spending several hours painting a large area, often at great risk. (As a noun, *tag* refers to a graffiti artist's name or initials. Some typical tags are Shame, Dr. Love, Speed 3, Chillie Willie, Spank, Ego, Lady 45, KM, Skeme, West, SG or Serge, OK, Stem, Stam, and Pleeze.) They have immense respect for the artistic efforts of others, and usually will not deface them or paint over them. The exception to this rule arises when two crews come into conflict and declare a "slash war" in which the object is to eliminate the other crew's graffiti. A slash war continues until the two crews arrange a truce "for the sake of art."

A slash war may occur under a variety of circumstances. For example:

> A lot of kids want to be in a crew but they ain't good enough writers. We call them toy writers. But they'll go and use someone else's tag or crew name and that's where the fighting come in. If you take someone's tag or crew name that's a very serious problem. Because you be fooling with their fame. And it takes a long time to get up [become known through graffiti], you know, so if somebody is using your tag you just wait on the train until they start to write and you find them and then you start kicking ass. That's your space and they are trying to steal it.

The mention of "fame" illustrates one of the chief goals of crew members, both individually and collectively. With the exception of crews that engage extensively in illegal activities like dealing in cocaine, most crews are looking for recognition—not only from peers but from the mass public. As Censor says,

> Most kids join crews because of the fame. If you get a permanent tag you'll get instant fame. Almost all the crews nowadays want to have a boogie [dance] crew and a writing [graffiti] crew. They want it because they can get the fame.

Underlying the craving for fame is, of course, the desire for personal respect and acceptance noted at the beginning of this chapter. The crew provides an identity and a means of gaining recognition for individual talent and achievement. Especially when the youth's environment is lacking in sources of potential recognition—at home, at school, and elsewhere—the crew fills the void.

Crews will accept almost any teenager who exhibits an essential trait: "street" (a code word for some intangible quality that appears to combine toughness with "heart" or "soul"). The following account, supplied by a Hispanic youth named Johnny Morales who has been a member of several crews, illustrates the background and experiences of a typical crew member.

> I was born in Queens fifteen years ago. My moms is Mexican and my father is Puerto Rican. I was raised in a pretty regular Spanish home. I have an

older brother, Luis, who is three years older than me. My folks have told me for years that I gotta respect my brother but I can't do that. Because when we were kids, he'd always bust my balls, man, trying to tell me what to do, how to do it, when to do it. He tried beating my ass, but I'd always fight back. One time I had a knife and almost stabbed him. Most of my scars aren't from the street, they're from him.

Both my parents worked while I went to school. When school was out, they allowed us to stay out and play until 5:30 P.M. See, my brother would always lose the keys. So, my moms got tired of it and said we had to stay outside till she came home. What I could never understand is why wasn't I given the keys. I finally got a set when I was 13. I have never lost them.

I always got along with pops. He's an ex-con and was in prison a couple of times while I was growing up. Now he works a regular factory job. He's not the greatest father, but who has? He don't live with us anymore. About a year ago he left for good. He and moms would always be arguing. If it wasn't about him staying out late, it would be about money. And if it wasn't about money, then it was his girlfriends. I'll never forget about how when a fight was a big one, pops would move out on moms, and then Luis and me would leave. We've lived in six different places since I was eight. It's a miracle I kept up with my own addresses.

As a kid, I was pretty bad. I started my criminal career at about nine. I was nine when I started to help my brother and his friends out. Since my brother was older than me, I used to try and always hang out with the big guys. They would always beat my ass. So did moms when she found out what I was up to.

Back then, I used to always go to school. I was pretty good then at going every day. I only started cutting out in the seventh grade. You know, you skip one class one day, and then another, and another until you start staying out for a day or two or more. That's why I ended up being left back. I was left back twice in the seventh grade. I'm supposed to be in the tenth right now, so I'm going to take a basic competency exam and if I pass it I get put into my right grade. The school I'm in now doesn't want me there for a third year.

I first started joining crews when I was 14 years old. That's also when I first got into real heavy jobs. The first big job I pulled was with the C.C. Boys. We took $400 from this doctor's office. Another time was a jewelry store, which was very profitable. Then there was this coke dealer's apartment where we got an ounce and $3,000 cash. We had to give 10 percent of what we get to the club, then the rest is divided by those that were involved. We also had the store at that time and it makes money too. For a while, I had a bank account with my mother as co-signer, but then I had to close it 'cause I started making more withdrawals than deposits.

The first crew I joined was the 78th Street Crew. They were a peaceful group and we just used to hang out and have fun. Right after that I was in the Latin Crew, but that only lasted two weeks cause they hooked up with Q.C. [Queens Connection] and I didn't want to deal with that. They should be called F.C. [Faggot Connection]. Then I got into the C.C. Boys. Boy, was I happy when I got accepted with them. The only problem there was I got arrested a couple of times and after three months decided to pull out. But it wasn't easy. I was kept tabs on for a while after that, just to make sure I wasn't being a traitor or double crew member. They're alright, but they're a hard crew. I wouldn't mess with them.

Once I was completely through with the C.C. Boys, I joined up with the Night Hawks. They were always getting into trouble. Someone was always getting stabbed, and since I didn't want to be next, I cut out. My mom used to also always get on my back about ending up in the joint because of them. So that was part of it too. From there I went into the East Side Nation. It was cool but everyone split up to join the bigger crews. I really felt at home there. It wasn't about color or being Spanish or Colombian or Puerto Rican, you know, it was everybody. After them, I hooked up with the J.H. [Jackson Heights] Crew and the M.C. [Master Con] Rockers.

Johnny joined one crew after another in search of one in which he could feel at home. For Johnny and many other poor teens, the crew is an extension of the family. It offers a feeling of kinship and the support of peers. Often, too, it provides a model, an authority figure in the form of a strong leader. Skeme, a 21-year-old crew leader who resumed his position after an interval of military service, is a model for numerous teenagers, not only in his crew but in several others.

The crew provides financial, emotional, and social guidance. It takes over some of the traditional roles of parents, guidance counselors, and other adults. Even the ethics of the crew—thrift, fight when encroached upon, mutual support in times of need, equitable sharing of profits and gains—are like those taught in the family. With few or no adults in their lives, crew members function without them except when they encounter the police, find themselves in trouble, or are in desperate need of things that parents or other adults can provide.

The crew is a haven for kids who are in effect marooned in the city. They are not being socialized directly or offered adequate opportunities to use their talents and energies. The crew allows them to deal collectively with whatever opportunities the city makes available. For this and other reasons, crews are more likely to develop in large cities than in smaller ones. The crews mentioned earlier are all based in New York City; in Cleveland, where mobility is lower and neighborhoods are more clearly delineated, there are groups like the Hell Raisers and the Mummies, but these are fighting gangs, not crews. The same is true in Mississippi, where roving bands of youth carrying baseball bats, guns, and knives occasionally fight youth from other sections of town over turf rights or minor incidents involving girls.

The crews in New York have a well-developed sense of PR and a strong desire to attract attention. Unlike peers who must stay home for lack of money, they have the excitement of ranging throughout the city with their friends. New York's extensive subway system is an important factor in the mobility of its crews. Instead of defending a geographic territory or turf, as the Cleveland gangs do, they compete for a mobile and fluctuating "turf": advertising space on the subways.

As a path to maturity, membership in a crew offers some advantages over the individual routes described earlier. In mimicking the structures of the larger society, the crews learn how to deal with that society. A disco crew, Grand Master Flash and the Furious Five, attracted the attention of a major recording company and has become a legitimate popular group. Some graffiti crews can be hired to paint signs and murals; individual artists have shown their works in galleries. The Cocaine City Boys have developed some of the skills required for business management. A crew known as Rock Steady promotes dances and the Electric Boogaloos specialize in robotic dancing. The Guardian Angels, whose mission is to help maintain safety on the New York subways, have gained a semilegitimate status in the public mind. Thus, for some ambitious young people—but by no means all—the experience of crew membership serves as preparation for a role in the world of adults.

7
Sneaker Mothers

> Be ready for responsibility and independence because it's something every woman and girl has to go through alone. And I think that once you have a baby you might as well get ready for a life, your life and someone else's life. You have to try to make a good life for both and to do that, no games and not too much fun, you have to be fully prepared to take care. It slows a young person down a hell of a lot.
>
> —a teenage mother

"Sex is a wonderful experience, a beautiful feeling," writes short, feisty Regina Eugene. "Making love can be extremely beautiful, especially if you have deep feelings for your sex partner. I have never made love to any man that I didn't have deep feelings for."

"Sex, it's a motherfucker," says Regina's friend Yolanda, "especially when you end up with a big stomach."

Both Regina and Yolanda are nineteen, and both have had "big stomachs." They are among the "sneaker mothers"—the 10 percent of 15- to 19-year-olds who become pregnant each year. There are a million others like them. Over 60 percent of these pregnancies result in live births, and in most cases the young woman decides to raise her own child. Usually she does not marry the baby's father.

The sneaker mothers do not consider themselves particularly sexual. For them, sex is part of a recreational pattern that also includes desultory TV watching, frequent marijuana smoking, and the consumption of vast quantities of pizza and pop. The following exchange between Regina and her "man," Vernon, is typical.

Vernon: Are you still going uptown?
Regina: Yes, later on.
Vernon: What time?
Regina: About two.
Vernon: Why so late?
Regina: Because I'm going to wash my hair, I'm hot.

This chapter is based on extensive research by Lorraine Mayfield among teenage mothers in Louisville, Meridian, and New York City.

Vernon: Why don't you come over here and wash your hair and do it in the air conditioner?
Regina: You going to come over here and get me?
Vernon: Are you ready?
Regina: No, but by the time you get here I will be.

(I got dressed and Vernon was here faster than I thought he would be; however, I was ready. We went into the cool house. We smoked a couple of joints and laid in the bed watching TV. TV watching led to love making.)

Vernon: I'm hungry.
Regina: What do you want?
Vernon: Pizza sounds good.
Regina: You going to get one?
Vernon: I guess I will.

(Vernon put his shoes on and left, I sat there and watched TV. When Vernon got back he cooked the pizza. We ate the pizza sitting on the floor acting silly. After eating the pizza, we sat on the couch and smoked a few joints.)

Teenagers like Regina and Yolanda have active sexual lives from an early age—sometimes as early as twelve. Part of the reason for this is lack of adult supervision. As one young mother explained, "I was given a great deal of freedom at an early age. My mother had left my father because he would beat her and my father would stay out of the house for days at a time. Although I had older brothers, I was able to go out and stay out as late as I pleased."

A far more telling reason than lack of supervision is a view of sex that denies its consequences. Teenagers in all of the communities we studied, while they are aware of the consequences of sexual activity, do not take responsibility for them. To them, pregnancy is a sort of occupational hazard. Nowhere is this more evident than in the following exchange between Regina and her aptly nicknamed friend Tiny:

Regina: Do you engage in sex?
Tiny: Yes.
Regina: Do you use protection?
Tiny: No, because I have been on pills for seven and a half years. The doctor told me I need a rest from the pills.
Regina: How often do you have sex?
Tiny: Four times a week.
Regina: Do you engage in oral sex?
Tiny: No, but I will when I get married.

These young women are not promiscuous. Almost without exception, they have sex with only one partner, usually a steady boyfriend. Tiny lived with her parents in a small wood-framed house in Louisville. She often skipped school to have sex with her boyfriend and would on occasion invite him over after her parents went to work. Going steady meant sex on a regular basis with him. For the girls, going out with one boy by age sixteen or seventeen was important socially because unlike the boys, the girls had to have one relationship at a time to avoid the stigma of being "fast." And in most of these communities being "fast" is one step short of being a whore. Sex is a way of pleasing—and in some cases keeping—a man. Often it is looked upon as a gift—a birthday or Christmas present. Our notes about one of the girls, 16-year-old Pestac of Harlem, illustrate this.

> Pestac first had sex in December after having dinner with her boyfriend, her close girlfriend, and her girlfriend's boyfriend (they all attend the same school). After dinner they went to a hotel. Pestac wasn't planning to have sex even at this point. She argued while in the room but decided to have sex thinking she was giving her boyfriend a "Christmas present." Before going to her hotel room, her girlfriend offered her one of her birth control pills. Pestac refused the pill. Up until this point, Pestac was a virgin. She didn't think about getting pregnant.

Pestac is a slight, quiet girl who dresses neatly and avoids the life of the streets. Yet like many other teens she neglected to take precautions against becoming pregnant.

Why do so many young women have sex without protection? Surely the sneaker mothers don't intend to get pregnant, at least not consciously. Yet 70 percent of them do not use any form of birth control. By and large, they are either uninformed or misinformed on this subject. They are especially hostile to the pill, claiming that it causes headaches, cancer, blood clots, obesity, ulcers, and a variety of other ailments. The IUD is accused of causing pain, excessive bleeding, and cramping, while the diaphragm is scorned as a "middle-class method" that interferes with sexual spontaneity.

As a result of this very widespread attitude, most of the teenage mothers are pregnant within a year after beginning their sexual lives. Only after giving birth do they seek a birth-control method in order to avoid future pregnancies, usually at the urging of their mothers and fathers, aunts, or sisters to "get something." Since the "something" is unspecified, the choice of a birth control method is often a difficult decision that is greatly influenced by the advice of poorly informed friends.

Of the young mothers we studied, 80 percent were using some form of birth control to prevent future pregnancies. This protection is often used intermittently or incorrectly, however, so that over 40 percent have had second pregnancies that were terminated by abortion.

The extent of misinformation about birth control is surprising given the fact that the majority of the teenage mothers have had a sex education course in school, and half of them received sex education before becoming pregnant.

Apparently it didn't sink in, as can be seen in the following comments by teenage mothers:

> Barbara, age 17: I had a sex ed course in elementary school. I was confused about some words and I don't remember any talk about contraception, only the pill.

> Linda, age 17: I found the course boring and I tried to cut that course as often as possible. I didn't know how it applied to my life. I wish I had listened.

> Cynthia, age 15: My teacher taught us about sex and birth control in a hygiene class. We saw some films, but that was it on the topic. We didn't spend much time on it.

> Janet, age 14: No one understood, but no one asked any questions.

A visit to a sex education class in a slum high school reveals the source of much of the teenagers' confusion. Often the class takes the form of a study period in which the students construct outlines from their hygiene books. Each student works individually; sometimes they whisper questions to each other if they don't understand a word or concept, but there is little opportunity to discuss human reproduction or birth control methods, and little interaction between the teacher and the students. Under these circumstances not much learning can take place. When teenagers do get accurate information about reproduction and contraception, it is usually from health-care professionals. But the sequence of events is usually pregnancy first, birth control second.

Since most teenage mothers do not intend to become pregnant, their initial reaction to pregnancy is shock and depression, followed fairly soon by acceptance. A typical comment is, "If God wants me to have children, there is nothing I can do about it." In some cases, however, there is a long period of denial—especially among very young mothers who have just begun to menstruate. In these cases acceptance may not occur until the third or fourth month of pregnancy, after a period of immense confusion. There are a few cases, also, in which the initial reaction is largely positive: "I was shocked, but happy."

Pregnant teenagers do not immediately share their feelings with their parents. More often they confide the news of their pregnancy to their girlfriends or sisters. Only after a month or so do they tell their parents. Sometimes the parents find out from other sources. Their daughters are afraid to tell them, and the girls' fear is usually justified by their parents' reactions to the news: "My mother and father argued at each other because I got pregnant. My daddy tried to whip me, my mother tried to work me to death."

In most cases the parents are very despondent about their daughter's pregnancy. By the time they find out about it, it is usually too late to do anything but anticipate having a grandchild. This prospect is generally shocking and disappointing, but eventually, if family resources allow, the grandchild is welcomed. Parental acceptance may be eased by the fact that in many cases the mother herself had her first child in her teens.

Once an adolescent learns that she is pregnant, she frequently has the option of getting an abortion. Overwhelmingly, the young mothers are against abortion, viewing it as criminal, sinful, or both. "I would never kill a baby" is a typical comment, as is "It's like going out in the streets and killing an old person. I think people should be locked up for having an abortion."

Some of the young mothers in rural Mississippi, where legal and safe abortion services are not available, are deterred by economics more than by ethics. As one teenager put it, "I think it's okay [an abortion]. I would have had one myself, if I could have gotten to Jackson. When I realized I was pregnant, it was too late. I was broke anyway."

For some pregnant teenagers, timing is the crucial factor in the decision for or against an abortion. Most abortions, particularly those using the D and C method, are performed during the first trimester of pregnancy. In New York State it is possible to have a legal abortion until the sixth month using the saline method. This method, however, is more expensive, more dangerous, and less available than the D and C. Thus, for most teenagers who consider an abortion, it must occur within the first three months of pregnancy. And as noted earlier, since many teenagers deny the fact of their pregnancy until after the third month, they are left with no choice but to bear the child.

If the pregnancy is not terminated (that is, in the great majority of cases), the young girl becomes a mother. In nine months she makes the transition from childhood to adulthood. Her life is transformed. Gone are the adolescent pleasures of going to movies, partying, spending money on snacks and clothes. Now she is responsible for preparing formulas, feeding her always-hungry infant, and taking care of it almost all the time. Instant maturity.

We do not use the phrase "instant maturity" lightly. For one thing, having a child is a symbol of maturity and (after an initial period of adjustment) is seen as such by the young mother's relatives and friends. Motherhood confers a specific identity where before there may have been only a restless searching; moreover, for better or worse this society regards motherhood as an occupation. This is an important fact in an environment that offers few alternatives to motherhood—a fact that is implicitly recognized by teenagers who postpone sexual activity until after they have graduated from high school.

For some young mothers, the rapid shift form childhood to adulthood is a positive experience. Carol J. of Meridian, a friendly, articulate young woman, is one of the fortunate ones.

> I had been working at a local nursery for over three years, so I had been saving money for [the baby's] arrival. I had moral and financial support from

my mother and the child's father. With their support I felt as though I could endure anything. Since we still had a close relationship, his support was vital.

My son Benjamin was born on May 20, 1978, at Anderson Hospital. Until I had gone through labor, I didn't realize my situation. It wasn't until we got home that I suddenly realized that I was a mother. It was a shock to finally see the baby that I had carried for nine months, finally where I could touch him. I had a good delivery, that took only five minutes. All through my pregnancy I read literature on babies, in order to strengthen my background on the subject. I wanted to know all about the do's and don'ts of baby care. After working at a nursery and saving my money, I felt that I could take care of my child or anyone else's child efficiently.

Now my son is 1 1/2 years old. He is steadily growing, learning, and surprising me each and every day. My child is my main motivation for living, because I want to provide for all of his needs. Each day he brings me love, laughter, and joy, and these things make my day brighter and fuller.

Never once have I regretted having my baby. I would never take a moment from my pregnancy. The pregnancy did complicate my life some, but to me it was worth it. Before I became pregnant I planned to join the Army to better my education and skills. These plans haven't changed, they were just delayed.

For most teenagers, becoming pregnant means dropping out of school. Even if they stay in until the baby is born, they drop out afterwards to take care of the child. Yet most mothers express a desire to complete their education—later.

A few pregnant teenagers transfer to special schools for pregnant students. These schools tend to be poorly funded and not very numerous (the five such schools in New York City serve approximately 650 of the 15,000 pregnant teenagers there). Their personnel is limited, and as a result the curriculum is also restricted. Thus the majority simply drop out.

Educators are aware that pregnancy is one of the main reasons that female teenagers drop out of school. In one high school we found that over 75 percent of the girls who became pregnant while attending the school did not graduate. The principal suggested that it is difficult to establish the pregnancy rate for teenagers who have already dropped out. An assistant principal called the surrounding housing projects a "baby factory" where many of his students had become pregnant in the preceding year. The health counselor expressed similar sentiments. Often, like parents, she learns that a teenager is pregnant in the third or fourth month, so that there are few options concerning the outcome of the pregnancy. Although the girls are able to continue their education at their local high schools, the teachers and school authorities do not encourage them to do so.

Many teenage mothers who drop out of school express the opinion that school is boring or that they are tired of it. Quite a number consider their fellow students silly, immature, and not really interested in learning. Adolescent parents who think of school in this fashion are unlikely to return to or remain in school. As one teenage mother put it, "After dropping out, it is difficult to get into the groove of school." An added factor for many young mothers is the fact that returning to school will mean repeating a grade before continuing.

In addition to these psychological barriers to continued education, the young mothers face economic and logistical barriers. Carmen's situation is a good example. Carmen is an attractive 18-year-old Puerto Rican mother with a six-month-old son. When we met her she was interested in returning to school, from which she had dropped out in the seventh month of her pregnancy. During the time she was pregnant she had left her mother's house and found an apartment, which she shared with her boyfriend for three months. Her boyfriend (who eventually left after a quarrel) discouraged her from attending school, saying that it was important for her to stay home and care for the baby. After he left, Carmen found a roommate, Angie, to share her three-and-a-half-room apartment. Angie was an 18-year-old mother with a eighteen-month-old son. Because of her responsibilities as a parent, numerous welfare and hospital appointments, and an active social life, Angie did not provide any help, either emotional or financial, for Carmen. In fact, within two months Carmen asked her to leave because she had not contributed toward the payment of any of the bills, including rent and electricity.

Carmen was left to run the household and take care of her baby. Her dream of returning to school became increasingly remote until she invited two male homosexual friends to live with her. For a while they were helpful. The run-down fourth-floor walkup was painted bright yellow and green. And 16-year-old Jose, who had dropped out of school, volunteered to watch the baby while Carmen returned to the local high school.

During a period of about two months Carmen left her baby with Jose and went to school, struggling to write book reports and do her math. Then she and Jose had a fight and she put him out of her apartment. She dropped out of school again, saying that she felt overwhelmed by trying to do everything herself.

Staying in school is only one of several major problems facing teenage mothers. Even more pressing is the question of how to make a living. Although most of the young mothers have a work history (that is, 75 percent have worked at either a part-time or a summer job), eight out of ten are dependent on public assistance for their support. Often the welfare check alone is insufficient to cover expenses. Some of the girls find occasional small jobs to do. Others are low-level drug dealers and hustlers of one kind or another. In addition, a kinship-based support system in low-income black communities provides either complete or partial financial assistance. In most cases the baby's father is unable to provide financial support because he is either not working or does not have enough money to help out.

Many of the young mothers have worked in fast-food chains as cashiers, food processors, or waitresses, or as clerks in local firms and hospitals, or as baby-sitters. But in today's economy even such low-paying jobs are scarce, and as a result most of the sneaker mothers are unemployed. Carol J. describes how it feels to be unemployed after having worked steadily for several years.

I have been working for Smith's Nursery going on four years. I enjoyed my job, working with the small children. Then in the 11th grade I became pregnant. In April, I got laid off. Being laid off is a terrible experience. I would never have made it, if I had not taken my mother's advice. My mother taught us to always save your money, look towards the future. I still have the same ideals.

I was laid off in April of 1978. I was without a paycheck for five months. I went to the unemployment office to see if I could draw my unemployment. The woman I spoke to said that "you must be able to work right now." Here I was, had been working three years at the place and can't even draw my unemployment pennies.

One month and two weeks later, I gave birth to a healthy 6 lb. 3 1/2 ounce baby boy. I still had no income for six weeks. After my six weeks were up, I went back to the unemployment office. This time I was able to sign up, but received my first check after three weeks of going down there for interviews. I was desperate for a job, but none was to be found.

When I finally got my check in June, my income was $112 a month. As hard as things were, every little bit helps. I lived off of unemployment compensation until the first week in September. In September, I went back to my old job at the nursery.

Another teenager expressed the meaning of work for a young mother.

When one doesn't have a job, it can mean being without money a lot of times. There are times when I may want to buy myself something or my baby, but I just can't. It feels pretty bad to walk in a place and want something you can't buy. It is frustrating to go look for work and don't find any. It even hurts worse when I try one particular job and fail, and someone else comes along and gets it.

When I don't have a job I have to depend on others. I hate to depend on welfare, because they only give you $60.00 a month for one child. My parents will help if I ask, but I like to be independent.

I wouldn't want a job as much if I didn't have a child. I like to be able to buy my child some of the things that she wants. I even like to buy little extras for her sometimes, but being jobless, I have to buy just what's needed. When one is jobless that means they can't even save for the future for themselves or family.

I keep hoping that jobs in the area will start hiring. I always go looking for jobs, and when there aren't any available, I feel better knowing that I tried. When I first became jobless it felt bad, but after a while I learned to accept it.

Even when jobs are available, it is difficult to find one at a salary sufficient to cover all of a young mother's expenses. Yolanda's experience is typical:

> I had a job as a clerk. I quit because I couldn't make enough to pay my babysitter and take care of my baby and me. I didn't think it was fair working all day away from my baby and then not making enough to buy anything, like food and clothes for me and the baby.

For most teenage mothers there is a threshold salary at which it becomes worthwhile to go out to work. Most of the jobs for which they might qualify pay less than that. Only one-fourth of the young mothers in our study had jobs. Usually they worked as typist-receptionists, clerk-typists, or waitresses. Many others expressed interest in obtaining a G.E.D. (equivalent to a high school diploma) and seeking out manpower employment and training programs in which they could learn a specific skill.

The experience of teenage mothers in training programs is generally unfavorable. Few such programs include child-care arrangements that facilitate all-day involvement by the mother. In addition, the programs are reluctant to accept pregnant teenagers and young mothers because they fear that these participants are more likely to have "negative terminations" and that they will be difficult to place. They also believe that parental responsibilities interfere with a teenager's ability to participate fully in such a program. In short, young mothers who attempt to enter job training programs often face discrimination by program officials.

Could all of these problems be avoided if the young mother married the child's father? The answer, in most cases, is no. As noted at the beginning of this chapter, it is unusual for poor teenage parents to marry. This is true for many reasons, not the least of which is the young people's own desire for personal freedom—freedom to date others, to continue their education, perhaps to travel or even migrate. The teenagers' parents also generally discourage marriage (forced marriage is unheard of), particularly if the baby's father is not working. In the background is the recognition that teenage marriages are often short-lived.

In reality, marriage has little to offer compared to the relative security to be found in the kinship network, usually combined with welfare benefits. Even if the baby's father has a job, it is usually temporary, poorly paid, and subject to layoffs. As a result, poor teenagers of both sexes tend to view marriage as a goal to be realized at some indefinite future time. As one young father put it—rather sadly—"I'm not ready yet. I still have nothing to offer you or my baby."

The result of this situation is that teenage fathers (if they are aware of their paternity) often enter the kinship network as friends of the family—

someone the young mother can call upon for occasional help. While there are some cases in which teenage parents live together, marriage is unlikely unless the couple's economic prospects are relatively secure. This point of view is reflected in our notes on Sue H., an 18-year-old Louisville mother who strongly desires a better standard of living.

> Sue had planned to marry Sidney, the father of her baby. He had been her boyfriend since age 15. Sidney is a 23-year-old high-school dropout. He moved into Sue's apartment as soon as she got it. At the time he wasn't working and couldn't provide anything for the household. Sue decided not to get married right away, thinking that she could do better on her own. She found that Sidney wasn't much help. Sidney has worked for CETA and helped with the bills. At present he is unemployed.
>
> Sue said that Sidney is considering going into the Army. She would like that and would consider marrying him if he did.
>
> Presently, Sue is not happy with Sidney, particularly since he is not working. Sue considers him lazy and would like to have him leave, although she doesn't want to put him out into the cold.

In the end, what it comes down to is the reality of the baby's presence. Sooner or later every teenage mother comes face to face with the fact that her life has changed and that the change is permanent. In conversations with these young women one often hears a note of wistfulness about their lost childhood. They often mention not having free time in which to participate in the activities enjoyed by their friends. At a deeper level, they are out of the mainstream of adolescent life. They spend most of their time caring for the baby—which translates into being virtually alone during most of the day.

When asked how her life has changed, a 16-year-old mother said, "It affected me in every way. I don't have no one to keep [my baby]. I'm young and I like to go out. I can't find a good man for staying home with the baby." Another young mother adds, "I don't never have time for myself, a baby always needs attention." And one of our community research assistants had this to say about her friend LJ: "She's a nice girl and everything. I mean she doesn't smoke, drink, get high or any of those things, but her mother doesn't let her go anywhere. All she do is cook, clean up, and take care of her baby. She's sort of like a modern-day Cinderella."

One result of this situation is an excessive amount of TV watching interspersed with time spent with the child. The following excerpt from the diary of a teenage mother is typical:

> The baby and I got up at 9:00 a.m. I fed her and played with her. By 12:00 she was asleep. So I took a bath, brushed my teeth, ate, combed my hair, and put on some clothes. And watched my stories [soap operas] on TV until 2:00. Then the baby got up so I gave her a bath, combed her hair, put some clothes

on her. About 3:00 I fed her again and watched some more TV and talked
with my grandmother. Around 4:00 my sister called.

Many young mothers, while they love their babies, describe them as
greedy and demanding. They are disappointed when the baby doesn't return
their love. This can be quite traumatic for a young woman who already feels
isolated from her friends (who are busy with school or work) and her parents
(who have not yet accepted the fact that they are grandparents). Often the
baby's father has discontinued the relationship and the mother feels abandoned. Carmen expressed these sentiments after her boyfriend left. She was
quite depressed and would spend long hours in front of the television set
watching the game shows, the "stories," and the afternoon movie. She took
care of her baby, but during this time she didn't take care of herself. She
didn't comb her hair, and she wore the same dark blue sweatshirt and faded
jeans every day. Sometimes tears came to her eyes as she spoke of the life she
was leading and her feeling that she had no control over it.

For some of the sneaker mothers life is not so difficult. This is especially
true if the young woman has the support of other family members—mother,
grandmother, sisters—who provide financial support, child care, and other
forms of assistance. While there are cases in which the girl's mother or grandmother takes over completely, in other situations the young mother and her
relatives are able to maintain a balanced, generally positive relationship. Such
a relationship can be seen in the following exchange between Judy Stone, a
resident of Cotter Homes in Louisville, and her mother:

(I went out on the porch, looked in the mail box. Both of my checks were
there. I went and asked mama to take me to the bank.)
Mother: Girl, don't you know, that is a blessing, you ought to really be
thankful. I be right back. You get the baby together while I get myself ready,
okay! (So I got the checks cashed, went to the store, put a few outfits in the
layaway. Went and ate lunch and rode around for a while, then we went
back home.)
Judy: Mama, I sure do thank you. Without your help I don't think we could
make it.
Mother: Yes, you could, honey, 'cause God is on your side. You could make
it without me. Don't ever say that 'cause you've got more than some others.
Be grateful, you hear! I'm going to take a nap. I'll talk to you later.

Despite all the difficulties they face, the sneaker mothers have surprisingly
positive attitudes about themselves. In a survey of twenty-five young mothers
in New York, we asked several questions aimed at discovering how they felt
about themselves. Among other things, they were asked whether they agreed
a lot or a little, or disagreed a little or a lot, with the following statements:

1. What happens to me is my own doing.
2. I am able to do things as well as most other people.
3. I have a positive attitude about myself.
4. I feel that I have a number of good qualities.

Overall, the respondents indicated that they felt very good about themselves and did not consider themselves less competent than older mothers. In general, they felt that they are more mature and better able to deal with the world than their contemporaries. Renee, a street-wise, self-possessed young woman whose appearance belies her youth, made this very clear:

> Although I am only 17, I feel that I am very mature. I have been on my own for a while and I've done most of the things that my friends are just beginning to do. I feel that I am a woman now. And I want to do the best I can for me and my baby.

Social workers who work with teenage mothers express concern about their emotional condition, their financial difficulties, their interrupted education, and the reactions and supportive capacity of their families. They claim that the teenagers perceive their children as "cute dolls" or possessions. The young mothers are not in touch with the emotional needs and developmental stages of their children. They may overfeed their babies, giving them cereal and whole foods before they can easily digest such foods. One of the major concerns of professionals is that teenage mothers have little understanding of what it means to be a parent, to provide for and love a child. For these and other reasons, greater efforts must be made to locate teenage mothers and assist them in overcoming the barriers they face.

The majority of the young mothers have a work history and know the value and importance of money in raising a family. Almost without exception, they look forward to completing school (usually via the G.E.D.) and going to work. Typical plans for the future are expressed in these comments by teenage mothers:

> I want to go to college and be happy and I hope to be married. But I can't go until I get someone to keep [the baby] because my parents work.

> I want to finish high school and get a job. I'll save some money and get a house in Puerto Rico to raise my family.

Other comments also reflect conventional desires—marriage, family, work:

> I want to have a healthy baby, get married, and go to college.

> I want to have a nursing career and get married with a family.

I want to get into business school to become a secretary and after getting training, get married.

Most teenage mothers want to work as nurses, secretaries, or accountants. Even when they are unsure of the particular job they want, they envision a life that includes work and family. The majority desire to complete high school, and 75 percent would like to continue their education either in college or in a training program. But returning to school takes on less importance if it will not definitely lead to a job that pays enough to cover both living costs and child care. Judy Stone's comments illustrate this point:

> I learned the lesson my mother was trying to get through my head all of these years. You don't get anything free, rather you can't get something for nothing. I know now you have to get out there and get it on your own. Up to now, I have been lazy, but not any more. I'm going to try my best to find something and go back to school on top of it. I really can't get anywhere without that piece of paper, which I have not got. So then maybe I can go out more than once out of a month, I mean really go out, eat dinner and go out dancing somewhere: have some spending money like I use to. I think I can do it if I really try as long as I keep in my mind who and what I'm doing it for. First my little girl, second myself so maybe we can go some more places that we want to go.
>
> I looked in the paper today, I couldn't find anything. Everything you had to have some kind of training. Like you had to have a high school education or training of some kind or I was too young.
>
> Being unemployed is terrible to me, nothing goes the right way, but I have to get out there and do it. Because nobody else is going to do it for me and I know that now. So I will go back to school and on top of that, when I get out I hope to get a typing job somewhere.

The most serious problem facing young mothers, thus, is not so much how to get into the labor force as how to get sufficient education and/or training to enter the labor force at a salary high enough to support the mother and her child and pay for child care as well. The motivation is there—almost all teenage mothers want to be self-sufficient and some, like Carol J., are very ambitious—but supportive services are lacking. Training programs often discriminate against teenage parents, and day-care facilities are scarce, particularly for children under three, making it difficult for young parents to participate in whatever manpower programs are available. Medical care is available, but teenagers are reluctant to take advantage of it—usually they show up only in an emergency. Hospitals and clinics attempt to reach teenage mothers, but this occurs primarily through the schools—and the young mothers usually have dropped out of school. In sum, although the problems facing teenage parents are numerous and severe, this group is hard to reach and keep track of.

8
Mentors—For Better or Worse

My idol was Watusi.
—Darryl Conway

I think it's because of Leroy
that I ended up going to college.
—A Williamsburg youth

It's a cool autumn morning in Williamsburg, Brooklyn. On Johnson Street, people move rapidly as if time were very precious. In front of a hand-made shack where dead cars are resurrected, two men struggle with a steel gate to the rhythms of Latin music emanating from an old radio.

The garage, as people call this dirty, oily, unimportant place, is the center of economic and social activity in the neighborhood. Almost as soon as the gate is opened, people stop by on their way to work. A car is dragged up the ramp for its last chance at existence. A husky little man comes to help his friends, who are already at work. His humble, almost whispered greeting is in Spanish.

"Hi Luis, hi Tony!"

"Hi Calilo, how are you today?"

Slowly Calilo begins to walk away. But before he has taken more than a few steps Luis stops him. Very politely Calilo asks, "Yeah, Luis, can I help you in any way?"

Luis strokes his beer belly and says in serious tones, "Listen, I need someone to get me a transmission for a Dodge van."

"What year?" Calilo asks.

Without hesitation Luis explains: "From 1967 to 1968. It has to be automatic. I'm willing to pay up to seventy-five dollars. But I don't want nothing hot from around here."

Calilo listens carefully and says, "OK. I'm going to tell the guys from Sheridan Street. Let's see what happens. OK?"

After a few hours Calilo comes back with two teenage boys from Sheridan Street. Luis repeats his instructions. Without saying much, the boys agree to the deal. They shake Luis' hand and depart. Their job will be hard and dangerous, but they know how to do it.

At three o'clock the boys from Sheridan Street drive up in an almost-brand-new van. Luis does not accept it because it doesn't have an automatic transmission. The boys take some expensive electrical equipment out of the van and leave.

Three hours later the van remains untouched. People are roaming around it. One can feel their hunger for the things inside it. Yet no one acts.

At half past six a few men gather in the garage for their daily game of dominos. Four of them sit around a table. Geronimo shuffles the dominos, and without a word each man takes seven pieces. For a moment there is complete silence. Then Ivan says, "Double six."

He places one of his pieces next to the double six. The other players look at him in disbelief. Smiling, Felipe pushes the domino back and says, "Chico, what the fuck is wrong with you?"

The game continues and more silly mistakes are made. There is an uncomfortable silence.

Finally Indio says, "Listen, why don't we empty out that fucking van?"

The game stops. The men look at each other. Doubtfully Geronimo comments, "But if we get caught, cono [damn], man, the cops can say that we stole it."

Felipe laughs.

"Cono, Geronimo, you know what's wrong with us? We are a bunch of pendejos [suckers]. We are scared of the police, the government, and the landlord. Shit, many of us think that the Americans are gods. Carajo [Hell]! We are the mamaos [suckers]."

For a moment there is silence. There is a battle in each man's heart. They all know that they want to empty out the van, but no one dares to take the first step. No one wants to spend any time in jail.

Tony, who has been listening while working, drops his wrench and blurts out, "God damn it! Are we going to empty out the van or not? What are we afraid of when there are so many of us? Don't we all need the money?"

They look at each other, and very seriously Corino says, "OK, OK, we are eleven. So let us all participate. Some of us watch for the cops while the others empty out the van. OK?"

Luis can no longer resist the temptation.

"Cono, let's do it. Que sea lo que Dios quiera [let it be God's will]."

Some watch while the others rapidly empty out the van. Indio calls his wife and a beautiful long-haired woman tucks her head out of the window. "Listen, baby," Indio instructs, "can you watch for the cops? I'm going to take some things out of that van."

She pleads with him: "But honey, don't you think you can get caught?"

Looking at his wife as if everything is all right, Indio insists. "You just watch and don't worry, OK?" Nervously, she agrees.

There are nervous movements throughout the block. People watch from their windows. No one calls the police. To do so would be to betray your people, your friends, or your family. The women and children help by watching and carrying some of the goods home. Finally the van is empty; even the tires are gone.

Now another decision must be made—the fate of the van. It is not needed, and legally no one is able to keep it. After some discussion the men decide to call the owner. A business card is found in the glove compartment. Someone calls while the others watch the van.

After an hour a company man comes looking for the van. He asks around to see if anyone knows anything about the missing goods. Nobody knows anything. The police come asking for information. Nobody has any. A tow truck comes and takes the van. The cops and the company man leave and the street returns to normal.

Most of the people who took part in the stripping of the van were adults, but the episode took place in front of everyone in the neighborhood. It became a fiesta—a public celebration of the people's determination to take what they feel they are deprived of by white society. This example was not lost on the youth of the neighborhood, especially since it developed out of the actions of a teenage group that was already deeply involved in criminal activity. For the people of Johnson Street, most of whom make a meager living at blue-collar work, the van provided an opportunity to get a little something extra. For the teenagers, it was another step toward involvement in illegal activities.

Direct examples of this sort are not the only way adults encourage hustling or illegal activity in young people. Parents are sometimes unwilling accomplices in their children's hustling careers. Take Darryl. Darryl's family was unable to keep him away from the street. His father was a small-time hustler whose advice during his infrequent visits from prison did little to deter his son from becoming a drug dealer. His mother often complained about the lack of money in the house, and when she discovered that Darryl was selling marijuana she looked the other way; in fact, she encouraged him to make money any way he could. Darryl's role models were not his parents but famous hustlers alive and dead. Those who chose him and other teenagers as runners were, from his point of view, helping him achieve his ambition to be like Watusi. It was not until much later in his hustling career that he recognized that they had been exploiting him—that he had been running tremendous risks in order to make someone else rich.

Other young people who are "on the street" and using "street smarts" may sometimes be directed toward adult mentors and legitimate careers. They are the teenagers who have found shelters on the street—places created by adults that act as informal learning centers for poor teenagers. An example is commonly found in gas stations in poor communities. The typical gas and service station, if it is not controlled by managers who live outside the neighborhood, becomes a center for the local cash and barter economy. Adult men who are not actually on the station's payroll trade in used parts, restore vehicles, swap tires, and perform a hundred small transactions. In many ghetto neighborhoods, where small factories are no longer plentiful and blue-collar work is scarce, the local gas stations, flat-fixing shops, and informal garages are among the only places where a boy can apprentice himself to someone who can teach him automotive skills. The youth may perform small errands, specialize in finding scarce parts or doing undesirable cleaning work on the cars, and eventually learn enough about some aspects of automotive maintenance so that he can market his skills. In this manner gas stations and similar businesses become shelters from the need to hang out with peers on the streets.

Most cash businesses, with the exception of the drug trade and other dangerous or illegal activities, can be considered shelters on the street. They give young people an opportunity to earn some money, learn about the work world of adults, and resist the temptations of illegal street activities or gang competition. But these shelters can accommodate only a limited number of teenagers, especially in times of high unemployment, when adults who are desperate for cash push younger competitors out.

Despite these problems, some of the young men and women who populate this book were saved by the opportunities offered by such shelters. One in particular, Alain Cooper, at the age of eleven found himself working as a cook, busboy, and dishwasher in a Harlem gin mill. There he learned a great many painful lessons about work and self-preservation, but those lessons contributed immensely to his ability to succeed in school and among his peers. For him, the bar and grill where he lost his youthful naiveté served as a shelter from possibly worse influences.

There are, of course, adults who care and whose influence on youth is entirely positive. They are the parents, teachers, coaches, youth workers, spiritual guides, and occasional employers who instill in young people the values and motivation that make the difference between a dead-end existence and a life with some sort of meaning. There is no better example of this special breed than Ron Searcy, Alain's teacher and mentor at Benjamin Franklin High School.

For someone like Searcy, watching a kid develop, mature, overcome disadvantages, and set out on the road to success is its own reward. The odds against such an outcome are extremely high, however. The subject of lost potential among poor youth is one that teachers and other helping adults seem never to tire of discussing. In every community agency and every school in each of the communities we studied, we found adults who expressed deep dismay about the number of young men and women whose lives appear to be wasted. Their inability to pay sufficient attention to the immediate needs and deficiencies of these young people hurts the adults almost as much as it does the youths themselves. "It drives me up the wall," a teacher in a Harlem junior high school lamented, "to see so many kids I could help achieve at grade level if I only had the time and the support to allow me to bend the curriculum and deal with them on an individual basis."

These adults are talking about 50 to 60 percent of the kids with whom they work. They are painfully aware that under present conditions only about one-third of those who could do well in school, or at school-related jobs, will have the opportunity to develop their potential. In some, this knowledge leads to burnout—bitterness, apathy, and a change of career. In others, it breeds increased resolve, even militancy. In a few, these feelings are combined in a frustrating blend of pessimism and hope. Listen to Willie Starkey, executive director of the Lexington Square Youth and Community Center in Cleveland:

> You know I just don't know what to say about the future of the kids here. You see the area and what it's gone down to. How can we give them any hope of living in this ugliness? Have you seen the Martin Luther King housing? You know that's only a couple of years old? Shoddy as it is and the city claims it's the fault of the families—walls falling in and all of that. There are no jobs available now for the parents, let alone the kids, with all the places shutting down. But something is bound to happen. Something has to open up. But my fear is it will be in job areas that our kids wouldn't know about. But if we could have extra people hired to research the job market and the requirements needed and then come to our kids with that information, then maybe some of the apprentice jobs that a lot of companies offer to young employees, but that they don't advertise, will come our way. The main reason these companies don't advertise is because they don't want to attract a significant number of blacks.

This sense of extreme frustration can also be heard in the comments of parents. Vern Hunt, a Harlem father, feels overwhelmed by forces over which he has no control:

> I have a 19-year-old, and you can't talk to him. He has a box [radio] in his ear. We are the last of a generation, and all of us here are 38, 39, 40. We are losing our people. They are having babies and not taking care of them as long as they have welfare.
>
> Our kids go through an educational system that is set up for white folks. So when you have your own system and we teach our children, things will be better. Because I go to school and I see the kids are fighting and I separate them and I say you are not supposed to fight your brother.

We are living in a time where that individuality is the thing. Do your thing. It is your thing, do your thing. And when the parents have that attitude, the kids are going to pick it up also. They want to do their thing, and they can't understand when they can't have this, if you got this. And they see you smoking pot, and they come up and they want to smoke pot. We are living in a system of things where everybody is out to do their own thing. Me first. You and everybody else second, if not third, fourth, or fifth. That is why the kids are so bad today. They want to do their thing. They don't want to respect authority. Because they learn from their parents.

What you have in this country whether you are white or black, the only thing is what your pocket does. If you work for a small company and steal money it is called embezzlement. If the mayor does it, it is called misappropriation of funds. If you are a big time guy and I come in there and drink, I am a drunk. But if I am a big time guy, I am a social drinker with alcoholic tendencies. It's all the same thing. How can you teach your children not to steal and it shows you on TV how to steal? How can you teach your children not to steal and the president cheats on his income tax? It is the same thing.

Art Lewis, who has two sons aged twelve and fourteen, concurs:

Nowadays, you care for your kids, but you see they have so many forces out there that they would rather go for than listen to what you are saying. The peer group is so strong. They got so many young kids around them who are smoking pot. They are hanging out. So most of the majority of kids are doing the opposite. So you want to put him in the Boy Scouts. You have to force yourself to push them in these organizations where other kids are not going. He is the only kid on the block that is going to the Boy Scouts, and the other kids are hanging out.

You know why they start all these programs? Because of the white junkies. When these white people were taking trips out of the windows, all these rehabilitation programs started.

What happened was it boomeranged. The thing was putting the drugs in the black neighborhood, but what happened was the white kids got a hold of it. Princeton, Yale, all the colleges, and all the places where the whites were. The white kids had the bread, so they got more of the stuff than they could afford. They had the bread. Look at Kennedy's son. If that was your kid, he would be in jail.

My kids are at home. My oldest boy is 14. I sit down and talk to him. I tell him I know you go to school and whatever you do outside, you do. When you get inside these steps, you leave what you do out there, and you don't bring no stuff in here.

I think it is a problem with the parents. Most of the black parents are not fully prepared to be parents. If they put all their efforts to seeing that their child has such and such a training, it would be different. Those outside influences are always there with any society. They have negative vibes, but once you instill the right thing in your child—I think I am going about what is right—the child will be alright.

Vern and Art are caring adults, parents who make every effort to instill positive values in their children. They feel powerless to counteract the negative influences of peers and other groups outside the home.

In every community we studied, we worked with young people who were well on their way to a self-destructive career in the undergound economy. There was little we could do for these young people, even though more sustained work with them and the availability of well-run programs might have eased them onto more productive paths. Yet the teenagers with whom we worked felt that they had "fallen into something good"—not because they were given anything material but because they were given attention by caring people.

Very often these caring people are simply friends, as Sandy explains:

> Friends play a major role in my life, because I feel that without friends you don't have too much going for you, and most likely never will. I used to be influenced mostly by the crowd, but something has happened since then. I still relate just as well. I'm influenced to do good in school by my parents. I want to show them that I can make As and Bs. I'm influenced by my sister-in-law too—she influences me to always try to look nice. That's because she always looks nice. That's the way I want to be. The funny thing about life is that you never know just what your life may bring forth. I feel God put us here for a purpose. Whether we see to that purpose or not is all up to us.
>
> I live in Cotter Homes, in some projects. It's in the west end of Louisville. Most people say that they would never live there. They say that it's too much crime, drugs, and everything else here. But if they'd look much of them things is everywhere. I don't regret being raised here. I feel it's been good for me because it's taught me to fight and stand up for what I think is right. It's also made me want to make a good life for myself too.

Sandy sees her youth in Cotter Homes as a positive experience on the whole; she has had to grow to be tough and to fight for her identity. She knows that she and her neighbors are stigmatized in the larger society, but she now has the confidence to insist on the positive values and the strength of the local institutions in her community. With greater opportunities for part-time and summer work, and with encouragement from her parents and improved educational programs, Sandy F. could be achieving at much higher levels. She is an intelligent and motivated young woman growing up in a high-density housing project area where there are scores of others like her as well as hundreds of others who are troubled and more likely to end up in distress or in dead-end jobs. Sandy has learned from experience that school achievement is her only route to the goals she seeks, and increasingly she looks for confirmation of her own values and goals in the support and encouragement she receives from family and friends.

Among the clearest findings emerging both from the young people's writing and from our field research is that young people are routinely faced with serious moral and economic choices. Vincent must make daily decisions about pot and drinking; Mack avoids crap games while presenting himself as a "regular guy"; the Cotter Homes kids in Louisville draw the line, so far, at heroin use and involvement in its sale; the Greenpoint boys are caught by the streets even after seeing one of their leaders gunned down. For these and other young people, the more opportunities there are to learn about work and have positive educational experiences both in school and outside, the easier it is to resist the temptations of the streets.

Given those temptations, together with the powerful pressure to conform to peer group norms, how is it that relatively few young people are caught in the fast life of hustles and the pursuit of pleasure? How is it that so many more manage to achieve in school, at work, or both despite all the odds? These questions are central to this study, but as phrased here they perpetuate the notion that there is a "fast track" and a "slow track" that youth fall into, depending on the examples set by their families and their own abilities and personalities. In fact, the situation is more complex. A very small minority of young people growing up in poor communities are sheltered from the influence of street life by their parents and community institutions like churches and schools. Another minority gravitate toward the hustlers' world at an early age and never leave. For the much larger middle population, the world of risks and highs and that of school and work are intertwined. The probabilities that teenagers will end up on the corner or in a stable job are conditioned by a great many features of life in their communities. Of these, we believe the most significant is the presence or absence of adult mentors.

One way to understand the diversity of the biographies presented in this book is to look at the paths to maturity that the various communities offer their teenagers and young adults. As discussed earlier, these are ways of behaving in situations defined by adults who establish standards and role models. These paths lead to specific careers in and out of the legitimate labor force.

As we use it, the term "career" does not imply choices about jobs, or even that a young person's life course is determined consciously. For some, like Ruth and Alain, the choice of a path involving school achievement and active participation in community organizations leads clearly toward college and eventual secure employment. And the choices these high achievers make are generally conscious ones. But for many of the other teenagers the choices are far more intuitive and subject to shaping by adults who have their own agendas for the kids. Indeed, the chief problem of many young people is that adult influences either are lacking or are of the type that steer them toward street hustles and the underground economy more generally.

The world of street hustles is a definite path to maturity. So are early parenthood, early employment at work that can develop skills, and success at supervised sports. The military is another, and the one that most clearly confers the symbols of adulthood on its recruits. Military service has the added advantage of taking young people outside their communities and involving them in an institutional setting governed by universal rules. But only a few of the young people we deal with in this volume could be said to clearly follow a given path. The majority are wavering among a number of possibilities. The directions they eventually take will most frequently be determined by the intentional intervention of adults who offer opportunities at the critical moment—or fail to do so.

Why did Darryl become a drug runner while Alain, who grew up under similar conditions and hardships, became a fledgling medical student? Why did Bones die of gunshot wounds while Biker stumbled in and out of work and drug programs? Why is Margo a hooker and Regina a teenage mother? These are difficult questions because they involve such complex interactions among social, psychological, cultural, and political factors. Of course, social class and family status are by far the most powerful variables in predicting the types of adult careers young people will have. In our study, however, the factors that separate the well-off from the middling and poor were held roughly constant. All the kids are from low-income households and poverty communities. Yet even within these communities, which are thought of by outsiders as rather homogeneous, we see tremendous variations in adult influences and the kinds of opportunities created by adults.

In Hough, Vincent at age ten was already a hardworking little boy, well supervised by a father who took him on long truck journeys. Vincent's path was reaching straight toward the blue-collar occupational world. Two years later, after his father's senseless murder, Vincent was depressed, confused, and only beginning to come around to his true character again, in part owing to the too-brief intervention of some people with a federal grant.

Rose, from the same neighborhood, lost her mother and had to begin fending for herself by the age of sixteen. Welfare payments provided her with income but not with a path toward maturity. That path was opened up by early motherhood and the influence of male friends who "turned her out" as a street hooker and hard-drug user. Rose is exemplary of young people who are existing on the margins of society in temporary living situations. The intervention at a critical moment of a program to assist young women like her can mean the difference between life and death, not only for Rose but for her two babies as well.

On Harlem's fast streets the biographies of Darryl, the flashy, successful drug entrepreneur, and Alain, the quiet, determined premedical student, highlight the difficulty of making individual predictions as well as the conclusion that among conditions that can be varied, the role of adult influence is essential. Darryl is following his adult heroes into the fastest lane of organized crime. Coming from a very similar background, Alain has rejected crime and is successful in school. Along the way he was assisted by a white teacher who paid him to do his primary-school homework; a spiritual mentor who taught him self-control and pride in his ancestry; his mother, who raised a large family herself and despite a long jail sentence managed to keep her family intact; and an assistant principal at his high school, who helped him on the way to college admission. Certainly there are elements in Alain's character that make him pursue different values than Darryl does, but a close examination of their biographies suggests that the role of adult intervention at critical stages in their lives made all the difference.

adult intervention

In their apartments in Cotter Homes in Louisville, Regina and her friends will fire up their joints at a moment's notice. Their lives seem to be an endless round of aimless parties, which often end in chemically induced sleep or sex and sleep. The few opportunities for employment are found in part-time work in burger joints or summer youth jobs. Their sense of the future is undeveloped, but the present has enough pleasures on most days to make that not seem such a problem. Here, among the thousands that could have been noted, is a group of young people on their way toward becoming the chronically unemployed underclass of tomorrow. This too is a path to maturity. Relatively free from constructive adult involvement, this path is toward welfare dependency and occupational redundancy. An ever-larger number of young people find themselves on this path.

Positive mentors for youth in low-income communities are among the most precious resources a community can have. Those who take it upon themselves to spend time with young people to whom they are not related are usually extremely altruistic. As the effort to encourage adult-youth mentoring becomes incorporated in social-policy initiatives, we would do well to try to understand the various motivations and roles, aside from pecuniary ones, that impel adults to work with young people in their spare time. In many instances the adult involvement that is included in the category of mentoring is motivated less by altruism than by a desire to find young people who will reflect well on the adult. Mentors for more troubled and less well-socialized young people are truly scarce. This point is well exemplified by adult involvement with kids in local sports organizations.

After mentors from the clergy, the schools, and formal youth organizations like the Scouts and the Y, adults who work with young people in athletic competition are the most numerous mentors at the community level. Sports organizations, including school sports, constitute a vast recruitment and sorting system, one that is closely linked to the world of work, as can be seen in this example from an interview with a prominent Meridian businessman:

When you came into my office I was just finishing a phone conversation with Coach _____ [the football coach at the senior high school]. Now, he has a black boy on the football team, a junior, who is a terrific fullback, 220 pounds, runs the 100 in well under ten seconds. Well, this boy is being heavily recruited by the Texas universities. But I want him for Ol' Miss, so I told the coach that and said we'd get that boy a summer job working on the Gulf oil rigs. He'll make over $9.50 an hour. We've just got to get him and I'm in charge of recruitment in this area of the state. I have boys in all my grocery stores who are on the major teams. We put the best football players to work in the meat lockers at almost $5.00 an hour and they build up their strength carrying those sides of beef. Some of the other athletes I put to work as clerks and warehouse workers at slightly above the minimum wage. All these boys, black and white, know that if they show promise I'm there to help them out if we possibly can.

Here, as in so many examples in all the communities we studied, adults with the resources to assist young people are involved in sports competition that gives the adults status in the local society. In Harlem, most of the boys we worked with had come up through the highly competitive summer basketball leagues. Only the most talented of them will ever play even at the high school level, but for the very talented few, sports are a certain path toward adults who can offer moral and material support.

Every summer some four thousand teenage boys are recruited into the Harlem Rucker Basketball League. There they receive coaching, adult advice, and in some cases modest wages for assisting in games for young players. Similar although less elaborate leagues exist in Louisville and Cleveland. For the Greenpoint boys, however, there is no opportunity to compete in organized sports. (There are Police Athletic Leagues, but the boys who hang out in the park have developed self-definitions that preclude involvement in police-related activities.) Again, for the most problematic teenage groups, mentors, even in sports, are generally absent. Where they are active, their role can be extraordinarily positive. For example:

> Leroy was a black dude who was maybe ten years older than us when we were coming up in Williamsburg. He really saved a bunch of us from real trouble. The dude worked full time in Manhattan but he'd round us up— the neighborhood kids, maybe eight or ten of us—and take us somewhere on the subway, or bring us to the park to play softball. He could speak Spanish some too. When we got in trouble in school or in the neighborhood he'd go to bat for us and later chew the hell out of us. I think it's because of Leroy that I ended up going to college.

One hears about people like Leroy again and again; indeed, where street mentors like him are not available the kids may seek them out. Thus, the Greenpoint boys asked William DeFazio, our field study director there, to take them to play softball and to show them around the city. But when one of the boys broke into his apartment it made all of them feel guilty and cut into DeFazio's ability to lead the group as a whole. He became a mentor for certain individuals but could not be a positive leader for the entire group.

Intentional efforts to supplement or replace parental efforts with adult mentors can be immensely successful, as was demonstrated by youth gang workers in New York and other major cities in the 1950s. But intentional efforts to support people like Leroy risk replacing altruism with pecuniary motivations. The most promising avenue for linking youth with adult mentors may therefore be through the schools and social-welfare agencies. The mentors they can recruit will be generally more limited in their involvement than people like Leroy, but they often have the ability to introduce teenagers to work settings and positive career paths, a vital aspect of socialization in the teenage years.

Of course, any intentional approach to the problems of low-income youth requires substantial resources, especially funds for developing effective new systems for training, mentoring, and job placement. Our ability to develop such systems has greatly improved over a generation of social experimentation, but our commitment to taking action in behalf of the least favored among us is fitful at best.

9
No More Rat Traps

> Them that's got shall get
> them that's not shall lose
> So the Bible says/and it still is news
> Papa may have, mama may have
> But God bless the child that's got his own.
> —song made famous by Billie Holiday

There's a certain sameness to life in the communities where poor youth live. It results from their common place in the socioeconomic order. All are communities where there is a concentration of relatively poor people, many of whom depend on welfare and other transfer payments for survival, while others depend on employment in social agencies and social programs, from day-care centers to weatherization projects. However, we should not forget that in these black, Hispanic, or old white-ethnic enclaves, a significant proportion of the adults hold stable jobs in metropolitan factories and downtown offices. The dollars they bring into the community make survival possible for all.

"No more rat traps" proclaims a poster in the window of the Hough Multi-Purpose Center. This is not a sign of political protest; it is a notice that a rodent control program for this beleaguered Cleveland community has run its course and will not be refunded. The Multi-Purpose Center houses a variety of community day-care, senior-citizen, and youth programs. It was built amid the rubble of the Hough riots of the 1960s, as was the adjacent Martin Luther King Recreation Center, a gathering place for teenage boys. Some of the 1960s militants also gather there from time to time, for strictly social purposes; militancy, for now, is discredited. Older unemployed men gather on the benches in front of the center and share pints of liquor ineffectively concealed in paper bags.

The Church's Chicken fast-food store near Louisville's Cotter Homes is almost always crowded. So is the one across 1st Avenue and 106th Street from the Metro North Projects in East Harlem. So are the McDonalds and Burger Kings and Shrimp Shacks in every one of the communities we studied. The adults are at work; visitors drop in and the youngsters run out to the fast-food stores, where very often they also look for jobs.

Every neighborhood park and bar-crowded street corner has its own group of unemployed and retired men. Unable to find a place in the labor market, they compete among themselves for a few shreds of self-respect. In the parks and sometimes on the street corners there are often groups of youth and adolescents. The men and boys may also meet in the social clubs, at the dog fights, or, at times, in the after-hours clubs, where the higher rollers of every age gather to relax and party.

And, of course, there are the churches: Baptist, African, Methodist, Episcopal, Roman Catholic, Pentecostal. The choirs, youth groups, and church-sponsored community organizations and action groups play a central role in the social lives of an important proportion of the community's youth. But every day the same churchgoing youth are exposed to the faster paced lifestyles of the street. There is often a great deal of overlap between the seemingly solid churchgoers and the world of hustlers, drug users, and sexual predators. All must share the same corners, the same schools and stores and playgrounds and other neighborhood institutions.

Much of the sameness of life in these communities is brought about by class and racial segregation. In Greenpoint, the white youth see themselves as living on an island populated by low-income white families and surrounded by a vast sea of black and Puerto Rican neighborhoods. In Louisville, Cleveland, and Harlem, the neighborhoods are segregated and there is almost no contact between black and white youth after school. In Meridian, the older southern pattern prevails. In this small city Afro-Americans do not live in large, segregated blocks, as they do in the larger cities; rather, distinct black neighborhoods are scattered throughout the town. In the rural hamlets and villages the same pattern prevails. The blacks live in small "hollers" or dusty crossroads, but never very far from white families, who are generally of the same class. Despite this greater propinquity, white and black lives are, with few exceptions, separate.

Other factors contributing to the uniformity of life for youth in poor communities are the absence of one or both parents, the low educational level of the adults, and, of course, the daily struggle to gain a living. Only 26.5 percent of the young people in our sample were living with both their natural parents; 56.2 percent were living with their mothers only, 2.7 percent with their fathers only, and 14.6 percent with neither parent. These figures differ somewhat by race and ethnicity, with 23.7 percent for white youth and 30.1 percent for Hispanic youth living with both parents. The most striking difference is the much higher rate of intact families among both blacks and whites in the Mississippi sample. This is an urban-rural difference that has persisted for generations. Even taking account of this difference, however, the modal family situation for disadvantaged youth is the single-parent, mother-centered home.

The Department of Labor's Youth Incentive Entitlement Eligibility Survey,[1] which our sample parallels, also looked carefully at the educational backgrounds of the teenagers' parents and at the sources of family income. The mean educational level of the parents of disadvantaged youth was 9.3 years, with Hispanic parents rating lowest at 8.3 years and black and white parents exhibiting equal levels of educational attainment (9.4 years). With regard to the sources of family income, a number of important points emerge from the entitlement survey. One of the myths that pervades discussions of disadvantaged youth is that they are typically dependent on AFDC or other transfer payments. The survey results show an average family income (in 1977) of $6,415, of which only $995 came from AFDC itself. In most of the sites where the survey of low-income youth was conducted, over 50 percent of family income was earned. AFDC payments were received by 46.5 percent of the families, and 70.2 percent received transfer payments, including food stamps. There is no question that public assistance is vital to the budgets of most disadvantaged people in the United States. Still, welfare and food stamps are insufficient to support a family. The important share of the family budget supplied by earned income, either that of children or that of the parents themselves, calls into question the stereotype of "welfare dependency." The entitlement survey shows that the survival of poor adolescents and their parents is predicated on work in the lowest paid, least desirable, and most insecure types of employment.

The parental status of teenage youth is a final dimension of the entitlement survey that deserves comment. The survey found that 23.3 percent of the young women and 14.7 percent of the men said they were parents of at least one child; 16.3 percent of the white females, 17.3 percent of the Hispanic females, and 25.6 percent of the black females were parents. At the same time, only 5.0 percent of the young women in the sample had ever been married, while 63.8 percent were heads of their own households.

Census data, together with other data drawn from the entitlement survey, provide some indication of the relative sizes of the youth populations dealt with in this study. When we look at the population most at risk, that is, youth who are not in school and not in the labor force, we find that New York City, with roughly nine times as many young people as Cleveland and Louisville, is in a class by itself. As a consequence of the absolute size of the neediest youth population in New York, that city's youth find the most creative as well as the most self-destructive ways of coping with disadvantage and deprivation. Cleveland, like New York, has experienced massive losses of entry-level jobs, and this phenomenon has its consequences in the relatively large proportion of Cleveland's youth who are out of school, on the streets, or incarcerated in detention centers and other correctional institutions. Louisville and Meridian are doing somewhat better economically, and as a result the youth populations in those cities that are at risk are small in both proportional and absolute terms.

The larger the city and the larger the concentration of poor and alienated youth in a given community, the more one finds anger and hopelessness expressed by the kids themselves. Poor adolescents often voice the opinion that they are part of a faceless mass, that they are not known as individuals outside their peer groups and immediate families. The more fortunate young people are those for whom there are family resources to draw upon and for whom there are mentors in the community who take an interest in them as people with names rather than as "disadvantaged youth" to be recruited for summer work or other programs. And the most fortunate are those whose innate abilities and motivation to succeed despite all obstacles allow them to do well in school and on the job.

When this study was being designed, a prominent *New York Times* editor suggested that we deal entirely with the problems of achieving youth in low-income communities. In this way we might be able to offer suggestions as to how these young people could be aided in their quest for education and constructive job opportunities. "By calling attention to the kids who get involved in hustles and street crime," the editor commented, "you risk perpetuating stereotypes about low-income kids. After all, in every ghetto there are hundreds of kids each year who do well in school. These are kids who need and deserve the limited breaks society has to offer."

We rejected this advice and chose instead to deal with the larger array of youth careers and lifestyles in low-income communities. It is true, however, that it would be a major social accomplishment if even the achieving youth in those communities could be assured of educational careers and job opportunities. It is possible to at least conceive of a society in which support for high achievers from low-income communities would not be mutually exclusive with support for all disadvantaged youth. The sad and undeniable fact is that neither group gets anything approaching the help it needs.

The economic and social institutions of impoverished central-city communities are incapable of caring for their neediest and most troubled youth under present economic and political conditions. The major private-sector corporations, especially those in basic industries, seem either too distant or under too much stress to provide employment opportunities for low-income inner-city youth. To be sure, some corporations could show much more leadership in the field of youth jobs, and in the long run local small businesses must play a central role in supplying jobs, but for the foreseeable future public-sector agencies and nonprofit concerns will also be a vital source of work and training opportunities. However, as this sector experiences the cumulative effects of federal and state budget cuts, much of the progress made in local institution building over the past ten years may be reversed. And since a large share of youth jobs in low-income communities are in the noncorporate sectors, the outlook for youth employment is likely to worsen. Opportunities in the underground economy, on the other hand—especially its more exploitive illegal branches—continue to flourish.

Our concern throughout this volume has often been focused on street youth, those young people who are living outside the networks of legitimate economic and social institutions in their communities. This is the group that is most difficult to reach and most at risk. Our policy recommendations are derived from what might be called a "continual opportunities for growth" model. To put it succinctly, disadvantaged youth require a constant supply of diverse opportunities for entry into the economic and social mainstream. Adolescents who fail in school, work in marginal (at best) employment, or drop out of the labor market as teenage parents, all need structures of opportunity within which they can realize their potential.

In all plans for "second chance" opportunity programs, basic literacy training is perhaps the most pressing overall need. In his extremely comprehensive review of existing and past employment and training programs for youth, Gordon Berlin of the Ford Foundation notes that for all participants in youth job programs, an individual's reading score at program entry was the best single predictor, with the exception of race, of individual gains in the programs. Based on his lengthy experience in the funding and design of such programs, Berlin concludes that strong literacy components must be established as part of any future approaches to youth employment and training. It is not sufficient, he agrees, to provide work alone. Young people who have not done well in school before, and who therefore are not adequately prepared for the new demands of the labor market, must have additional chances to gain literacy. There is growing agreement that this need outweighs even the potential benefits of work itself, although when work and basic skills learning are connected they increase the likelihood that young people will make substantial gains in future earnings.[2]

As noted throughout this book, however, the most salient characteristic of the opportunity structure encountered by young people today is the absence of legitimate employment opportunities. This situation can only be described as "social dynamite." Our experience with young people in seven low-income communities offers ample evidence of the impact of job shortages. The links between worklessness and juvenile delinquency or teenage pregnancy are not difficult to identify. The problems posed by inadequate preparation for work, and by competing alternatives in the illegal economy, are certainly real, but they are relatively minor compared with the absolute shortage of jobs.

One of the nation's most experienced students of manpower statistics, Dr. Eli Ginzberg of the National Commission on Employment Policy, notes that when he and his colleagues began studying the youth unemployment problem in the late 1960s they "came to the conclusion that the dimensions and effects of black youth unemployment constituted not merely a serious problem but a real crisis. A decade later the crisis persists. A social and economic crisis of ten years duration must surely be considered a catastrophe."[3] This grim conclusion is based on the persistent finding that while the national rate of youth unemployment for whites (age 16–19) has fluctuated around 11 percent over the last few years, the same rate for black youth is about 33 percent. And when one looks not at the official unemployment rate but at the ratio of employment to population, the overall ratio for white youth in the late 1970s was 61 percent while for black youth it was only 33 percent. Ginzberg also observes that in some ghetto communities the youth unemployment rate may exceed 40 percent.

For the nation as a whole, private-sector jobs generally account for 80 percent of employment of people between the ages of 16 and 20. In our study communities, however, there is a great deal of variation in the availability of private-sector work. In Meridian and the surrounding villages, the private sector accounts for at least 80 percent of whatever youth employment there is. The same holds for Greenpoint. In the other communities, however, private-sector work accounted for less than 45 percent of jobs among young people with whom we had contact. It is clear that some communities require more governmental assistance in job creation for youth than others. A single approach that stresses the role of the private sector cannot work well everywhere.

Legislative policy deliberations often lump youth between the ages of 16 and 20 into one age category where public employment policy is concerned. But this is hardly a relevant age grouping for private employers. Nor does it correspond very well to the way young people behave with respect to the job market or other aspects of their lives. The 16-year-old prospective employee is generally closer to the 14-year-old in life experiences and emotional maturity than to the 18- or 19-year-old. Experience with work and earned income figure prominently in the development of individual maturity, and there are striking similarities in adolescent maturation that cut across class, racial, or ethnic groups.

"You have to remember how shy and timid kids can be," observes an employment counselor from Cleveland's East Technical High School, which serves the Hough community. "Boys and girls who can dress up and go alone to a strange employer in a strange community to ask for a job have already demonstrated a level of maturity you don't see that often in kids of sixteen or less." The youth in our study who wrote about their early efforts to earn money by running errands and hanging around stores tend to be early maturers from a labor-market perspective. The exposure of these young people to work settings often leads them to seek regular work as soon as they are old enough to obtain working papers. But boys who are less outgoing and have not been exposed to the world of work in their preadolescent years usually find it extremely difficult to obtain private-sector jobs on their own. This difficulty is even more serious among teenage girls. In every neighborhood we studied, young teenage females were less mobile than their male counterparts. The girls were consequently far less likely to have had early experiences with wage work in private business.

Young teenage girls are in demand as baby-sitters, but until they are at least seventeen it is extremely difficult for them to find any other type of work. In some neighborhoods we found fifteen- and sixteen-year-old girls working part time in bakeries and other small retail concerns where counter assistance is needed. In communities such as those we worked in, however, the number of such jobs in relation to the demand is inadequate. As a result, parenthood and domestic responsibilities are the primary skills the girls learn and the most visible path out of childhood. This is as true for white teenage girls in Greenpoint as it is for minority girls in any of the other communities. Without some sort of channel to the labor market, the average girl from a poor urban family has relatively little hope of finding a wage job that is accessible to her. Despite the fact that such jobs may go begging in communities beyond her own world of experience, she will typically remain in a child-centered social milieu. Her contacts with the larger social world will depend on her relationships with boys and young men. Among other misfortunes, this dependence on males helps to establish the conditions leading to high rates of juvenile pregnancy.

The difficulty of obtaining private-sector employment for youth in poor communities in the 1970s led the Department of Labor's Office of Youth Programs under the tireless leadership of Robert Taggart to propose that each eligible teenager be assisted in compiling a personal employment development plan. This would permit job counselors and prospective employers to determine the readiness of each young person to take on added work responsibilities. Implicit in this proposal was the idea that federally subsidized work should provide a bridge to more permanent employment in private industry. With a more systematic assessment of a young person's "world-of-work readiness," the job placement process would be more rational and public-sector employment could be more effectively targeted for younger teenagers who were just beginning to enter the labor force as summer and part-time workers. Without this sort of placement process, poor teenagers who lack adult sponsors tend to remain in public summer youth employment longer than is good for them, the programs, or the private-sector labor market.

In the summer of 1980 there were close to 100,000 applications for federal summer youth work in New York City alone. Only 54,000 positions were actually available. For the summer of 1981, New York City received funds for 48,000 summer jobs, a cut of 11 percent. Similar reductions occurred in most other large cities. Reductions of this magnitude make it even more urgent that greater efforts be made to target jobs for younger teenagers who can benefit most from federally funded summer work. Recruitment of youth in the private sector, on the other hand, needs to be directed toward older teenagers, who are more likely to have exhausted the potential benefits of subsidized summer work. Older teenagers are also more likely to be able to convert summer work in private business into longer-term jobs.

Despite the obvious need, the current political climate in Washington is one of vacillation between pleas for quick fixes and more systematic efforts at institution building in the field of youth employment and training. Thus, on the one hand the Reagan administration proposes "solutions" like the subminimum wage for youth and the idea of creating economic development zones in depressed areas, and on the other it tries to encourage Congress and local governments to build up the role of partnerships between public-sector agencies and private businesses in the provision of work for young people. The encouragement of local job-creating partnerships that involve business in youth employment and training continues and strengthens a trend that began in the late 1970s. It represents a continuation of efforts to build social programs at the community level that will develop ever more effective combinations of employment and training opportunities. But at the same time the Department of Labor has downgraded the Office of Youth Programs and effectively abdicated its previous leadership role, leaving local and state governments to fill the vacuum as they see fit.

The importance of the partnership approach is that it helps ensure continuity, at least at the state and local levels, in efforts to develop jobs and occupational training for young people. The difficulty with proposals like the subminimum wage, on the other hand, is that they detract from the more difficult planning and negotiation processes whereby effective partnerships are formed. Although motivated by a genuine belief in the free market and free-enterprise mechanisms, these policies run counter to massive evidence, accumulated over years of experience, showing that disadvantaged youth require the assistance of governmental subsidies, educational programs, job training programs, and an array of other services to help them overcome the many obstacles standing between them and private- or public-sector employment.

The debate over the minimum wage is a case in point. Any discussion of job creation in private business and industry immediately raises the issue of the impact of minimum-wage requirements and the possible effects of a subminimum wage for youth hired in the private sector. "In my opinion," says the owner of a food-store chain in Meridian, "the minimum wage is most detrimental to the hiring of high school kids in summer, on weekends, and after school. If Congress would see fit to let us hire a kid at $2.50 rather than $3.25, I think you'd see a lot more kids hired."

This view is characteristic of the opinions one hears expressed at meetings of business associations. But the businessman just quoted went on to explain that with regard to "your high school dropout and unemployed after high school kid . . . I am not for federal rules and government interfering with business, but if Congress would pass some kind of incentive for business to hire this kind of individual, and that they would subsidize me, I think you'd see that we could make it go." He did not know that Congress had already passed such legislation in the form of the Targeted Jobs Tax Credit program and that he could receive a subsidy in the form of tax credits for employing disadvantaged youth. We heard similar opinions from businesspeople in all the communities we studied. There is a good deal of confusion about the concept of a subminimum wage and a great deal of ignorance about existing subsidies for private industry, both of which are indicative of a lack of certainty that a "youth wage" would actually produce the desired results. This is why businesspeople often suggest that some form of subsidy might help them create youth jobs as effectively as a subminimum wage.

There are a number of problems with the youth wage concept. Among them are the following:

It could have serious political consequences. It creates a second class of youthful workers, some of whom may already have earned income at the minimum wage. Individuals who are subject to youth wage legislation are voters and potential voters.

The youth wage concept assumes that youth themselves should pay the "on-the-job" training costs usually paid by employers or by society, a form of age discrimination inherent in the legislation.

Job creation resulting from youth wage legislation need not have any direct bearing on the availability of jobs where they are needed most.

The youth wage permits employers who routinely employ youth at the minimum wage (for example, in short-order franchise restaurants) to reduce labor costs with no resultant saving to the consumer or advantage to society in the form of tax revenues.

The subminimum wage fails to offer youth enough incentive to venture out of their communities in search of work.

In short, because it would effectively legalize labor market segmentation, the youth wage proposal is unintelligent politics and hence is unlikely to come about. Unfortunately for laissez-faire policy makers, the probable failure of the youth wage and the simultaneous exclusion of over one million young people from the regular economy as a result of the termination of federally subsidized jobs and training programs leaves a generation of teenagers with precious little to look forward to but economic insecurity and fierce intergroup competition.

For decades social scientists have been insisting on the central role of public policy in dealing with these issues. Yet in every city in which we worked we heard a powerful alternative viewpoint, a distinctly American outlook on these questions. Many of the most successful business, social, and intellectual leaders of these communities and of the nation see the inability of poor blacks and whites to gain economic mobility as largely a failure of their own social organization and collective determination. A prominent oilman and community leader in eastern Mississippi expressed this viewpoint to us quite directly:

> I tell my black neighbors, Lincoln set you free but you're in a worse state than you were. You're ending up on a concrete reservation. You're becoming wards of the state. They're convincing you that you can't do anything. You need to get into business. You need education.

Of course, this viewpoint takes many more sophisticated forms, from prescriptions for benign neglect to exhortations that blacks and other minority groups follow the patterns of community building established by white ethnic groups. But in all of its versions the underlying theme is that overdependence on the institutions of the welfare state are a significant cause of the condition in which the poor find themselves today. Fortunately, in our study we worked with enough of a cross section of poor youth and involved adults to be able to generalize some of our findings and prescriptions beyond one race. We also had occasion to see the degree to which this increasingly common viewpoint contrasts with the actual behavior and attitudes of poor people themselves.

The best way to make this point is to evaluate the experience of adolescents in subsidized programs. Regardless of whether the jobs involved are in the private or the public sector, the same general questions about their impact as subsidized work apply. The most global question, and the one most subject to ideological debate, is whether young people in federally subsidized work and training programs benefit from these investments of public funds, that is, whether they are able to make the transition from subsidized to nonsubsidized work as a result of their participation in the programs.

In general, our assessment of youth experiences in federal youth job programs supports Cleveland councilwoman Fanny Lewis' assertion that all of the federal programs have "done some good." But how much good and for whom and with what lasting consequences for youth participation in the labor force? These are fair questions, to which we can provide some tentative answers.

Work experiences in which teenagers have mentors who teach work skills are more effective than programs in which young people work in larger groups. The exception to this general finding is where citizenship attitudes are concerned. Surprisingly, the much-maligned group work in public facilities does seem to develop better citizenship attitudes. These findings are confirmed over and over again by the young research assistants who worked with our study team. It is also based on direct experience by our field study directors in youth employment programs. "Effective" in this context refers to a number of important outcomes. Among these are the probability that young people will find work outside of subsidized employment programs as a result of their experiences; that they develop world-of-work skills, and especially a positive attitude toward giving a fair day's work for a day's pay; and finally, that the young people experience heightened awareness of their rights and obligations as citizens. With these criteria in mind, let us summarize the experiences of the young people in our study communities with the most common subsidized work programs.

Summer work sponsored by federal funds and channeled through state employment agencies and municipal sponsors is by far the most important source of work experience for youth in low-income communities. Slots in the federally sponsored summer youth employment programs number in the thousands in the cities where we worked, while slots in the year-round employment programs under the Youth Employment Demonstration Projects Act (YEDPA), the Comprehensive Employment Training Act (CETA), or the Jobs Training and Partnership Acts (JTPA) number in the hundreds. In low-income urban areas, no other source of employment begins to provide as many temporary jobs for youth as summer youth work funded by the U.S. Department of Labor. Since the CETA and YEDPA school-to-work programs have been ended under the present administration, summer work programs remain the only substantial youth work program sponsored by the federal government.

There are two main types of summer youth employment subsidized by Department of Labor funds. The first consists of employment situations in which teenagers work in crews of ten or more workers under the direction of young adult supervisors. These summer work situations usually involve outdoor conservation and cleanup in housing projects, parks, streets, and other quasi-public spaces like cemeteries and schoolyards.

The second prevalent summer work situation involves youth workers in individual or small-group assignments, usually in public-service agencies like day-care centers, municipal agencies, and community-based organizations of all descriptions. The latter are typically local churches and civic voluntary associations that have contracted for a small number of summer workers from their local sponsor, or voluntary agencies whose activities are community-wide or even municipal in scope. In most cities the sports leagues are a good example of youth agencies that employ summer workers to supplement adult organizers. In Harlem, for example, the extensive youth basketball leagues organized by the Harlem Rucker League and others employ summer youth workers to assist in the organization and operation of sports competition. Through the efforts of these leagues, a small number of workers help organize the vacation activities of thousands of teenagers and preadolescents.

Approximately 80 percent of the young people in our study had one or more summers of experience in federally subsidized work. Indeed, summer employment is the prototype of subsidized work in the minds of most poor adolescents. More ambitious employment programs like Neighborhood Youth Corps, Young Adult Conservation Corps, and Youth Employment Training Programs often become confused with summer youth employment when the young people fill out job applications or resumés. But of all these programs, summer youth work requires the least additional world-of-work training, gets by with the highest ratios of youth workers to supervisors, and applies the most equitable employment criteria. Since it is the largest of the youth employment programs, it is least subject to local patronage politics, selection of youths with special skills ("creaming"), and nepotism.

As mentioned earlier, our study combined ethnographic research with an employment demonstration. The results of the demonstration are instructive in the context of the present discussion. Every young person who completed his or her term of employment with us gained valuable work experience and improved interpersonal skills, which can be expected to be tangible advantages in future job searches. The most rewarding aspect of a youth employment demonstration, however, is seeing how quickly young people can overcome years of disadvantage in education and life experiences, how quickly they can become competitive in the larger labor market, and how rapidly their literacy can improve under intensive training. These kinds of gains at the individual level were an important result of the demonstration.

All of the community research assistants who stuck with the demonstration made perceptible gains in world-of-work skills, literacy, and self-sufficiency. Those who had only limited experience working for an official employer (as opposed to work in the underground economy) learned to account for their time both on the job and off it, to notify their director whenever they had to be late, to obtain a doctor's note whenever illness prevented them from being present at more than one group meeting, to turn in their work on time, and to improve the quality of their written work. In general, we estimate that the young people advanced an average of one grade level as a result of their relatively brief participation in the demonstration. Teachers' reports in each of the cities corroborate this finding, and many of the teenagers actually advanced well over one grade level in their writing skills.

The fact that we required the boys and girls to revise their life histories over and over again not only led them to improve their writing skills but also caused many to gain new insights into their feelings about themselves and society. Here is a segment of the life history of a teenager from Williamsburg that exemplifies the kind of renewed self-pride and facility of expression that often emerges from this work. This boy was at risk of becoming a school dropout before he became involved in the demonstration. His writing skills were at the fifth-grade level. Although this effort could not be graded beyond the eighth- or ninth-grade level, it represents a vast improvement over what the youth was able to produce when he began writing:

To be black is to know, understand and love. To know that we must strive on to a world of peace as others before us have tried and made the way a little easier and a little less painful for the others to come. To be black is knowing and remembering our people before us and what they went through. From slavery to where we are now we must remember how we got to this point in life. Why without the people, or should I say leaders, we might still be in the cotton field. We as a people have progressed but we must not stop now. We must progress on to a better world.

To be black is to hold our pride as precious and to keep on keeping on. We must see that day when we have peace. To be black is to have that feeling of progress, to want to be a better people. One day we want to be able to repeat the words of Martin Luther King, Jr.—"Free at last. Free at last. Thank God almighty, we are free at last." We must in turn become leaders to help those who are slow and might wander off the road. And we will lead. We must prepare the way for our younger brothers and sisters and teach them so that after us they will lead. Because the road to freedom and peace is a long and trying road.

We as black people care about each other and we are always trying to help each other. And if we can continue along this basic path we will make it with God's help. We must never forget our heritage, how our forefathers were treated by the white man. We must never forget how we came to be the people we are today. We must keep our faith in God for he helped us to where we are now and he will help us move on.

Being black is also fun. We know how to go out and have a nice time. We party, have reunions, rap sessions and everything. At rap sessions we sit around and talk about whatever comes to mind. At parties we get together to have fun like dancing, talking, and simply bugging out when it comes down to the younger generation. We dig jazz, soul, disco, etc.

We are always together. Whether family or friends we are always having reunions. Bus loads of family come to each other's house for Thanksgiving, Christmas, and many other holidays. At these reunions there is so much to eat. What do we eat? Well there is so much that I only have room to list a few. There is cakes, pies, pig feet, ham, collard greens, chitlins, potatoes, salad, turkey, chicken, cornbread, biscuits, etc. I'll tell you one thing our people sure know how to cook.

Being young and black (Afro-American) means this and a great deal more to me. But there is just so much you can put on paper and be understood. But one thing for sure, we will keep on keeping on . . .

Freedom will be obtained when everyone black, white, Puerto Rican, etc. will be considered and treated equally. When we can all work, talk and live together as one. When we can go get a job without considering your race. When races can be forgotten and we all treat everyone as sisters and brothers.

Freedom can be obtained by caring for everyone a little more. Trying our best to help everyone and share with everyone. By forgetting that we have enemies and try to resolve those problems between us.

If everyone who hates minorities really sat down and thought about their hate they will see that there is no reason to hate. They will see that their forefathers hated us black people and kept us as slaves. They hate just because they were taught how to hate. I feel if we stick together and overcome all the wrong and mixed up emotions, if we overcome hate, poverty, etc. we can make this world a free world.

We are confident that the teenagers employed in the demonstration gave a fair day's work for their pay, and that individuals gained skills, self-confidence, and knowledge from their work experience. But what are the gains for the larger society and for the communities where the demonstration was implemented? We cannot be at all sanguine about such gains because most of the programs to which our research assistants might have added their new skills are gone. Vital educational programs in the areas of sex education, world-of-work training, science education, and many others are under severe attack. At the same time, juvenile crime remains at extremely high levels and the illegal economy is booming.

Most adults in low-income communities feel that the situation of their children will get worse, with extremely negative consequences for the larger community. In the 1950s and 1960s, when teenage gang activity became a serious threat to the safety of the more affluent, trained street gang workers were sent to work with youth in the most troubled communities. Often their efforts enabled young people to get themselves out of a developmental path that was leading them toward a possible early death or certain imprisonment. In the late 1960s and 1970s, drug treatment programs were organized to deal with the plague of heroin and speed addictions that tore apart entire neighborhoods in cities and suburbs. Few such initiatives are now being made to cope with chronic youth unemployment and renewed gang activity.

The efforts of our field study directors in the area of youth employment were analogous (on a small scale) to the activities of earlier gang workers and drug-treatment organizers. Through them we developed contacts with the major groups of teenagers in the study neighborhoods, from the most troubled to those who were seeking to avoid trouble and to achieve in the mainstream institutions of society.

For the communities in which the demonstration took place there were also some gains. The development of a cadre of local youth, each of whom was in touch with a larger network of peers and acquaintances, created the potential for more effective implementation of youth manpower programs in the future. Once a few young people learn about the range of opportunities available both in training and in actual employment, and are trained to understand the networks of youth and helping adults in their communities, they can act as effective recruiters. This is particularly true with respect to outreach to school dropouts and teenage mothers, two of the groups that are the most difficult to draw into employment and training programs. During the course of our demonstration there were numerous examples of young people functioning as informal recruiters, and in fact many of the teenagers whom we eventually hired were initially recruited by young people who were already working as community research assistants. How the youth networks that developed as a consequence of the demonstration might have functioned over the longer term is a subject about which we can only speculate, since it was not possible to obtain resources to further develop this aspect of work with local youth.

In a short survey conducted by Field Study Director Jose Figueroa among 150 summer youth workers assigned to his community in Williamsburg, 85 percent of the youths said they felt that their work had made an "important contribution to building the community." An equal proportion said that when they began their work they did not believe their efforts would have any beneficial effects on the community. The young workers had assimilated the negative evaluation of subsidized summer work that they hear expressed everywhere. And over the course of the summer these teenagers experienced all the common problems of summer youth program workers. There were violent confrontations between supervisors and workers, demands by workers to be transferred away from their home housing projects so that friends who were simply hanging out would not taunt them, and endless incidents of harassment of female workers. Extremely little effort could be given to teaching the young workers the value of the cleanup work around their Brooklyn housing projects. Little time could be devoted to instructing individual workers in how to rake or sweep or erase graffiti. There were no discussions between residents of the projects and the young workers about tasks that needed to be done. Despite all these missing ingredients, the young workers felt that they had made an important contribution to the community.

The enhanced sense of citizenship gained through even the most average outdoor work in an urban summer employment program indicates the potential benefits to be derived from youth employment in public works. If individual employment is more likely to bring a young worker into contact with a mentor who can teach about the world of work on a firsthand basis, group work outdoors has the potential for conveying a much greater experience in citizenship than is possible in, for example, individual office employment. The experience of citizenship, the enhanced feeling of belonging to a community and working to make a contribution to the betterment of that community, is a dimension of youth employment in manpower programs that is not anticipated in labor market theories. Enhanced citizenship needs to be measured more carefully in the future and institutionalized in the programs themselves, even if it requires greater investment in preprogram design, direct supervision, and evaluation. To waste the citizenship training potential of summer youth employment, to regard these jobs merely as part of the "social safety net" or a form of "workfare," is to squander perhaps their most unique contribution to society.

Young workers and students who are about to drop out or graduate from high school and seek entry into the labor force face an extremely uncertain future if they do not have adequate scholastic skills or marketable occupational skills. There is widespread confusion among labor experts about the impact of the new computer-based technologies. Will they produce more jobs than they eliminate? Will young workers who cannot compete for more sophisticated technology-based jobs find themselves chronically unemployed or relegated to marginal employment? No one can yet answer these questions satisfactorily, but there is general agreement that our society will increasingly need to invest in the development of its human capital, that it will have to make special efforts to save this generation of late-baby-boom children from suffering continued severe difficulty in access to jobs with careers. To accomplish this, we believe that eventually the nation will need to establish a system of national service that is compulsory for all young people.

Long a dream of those who remember the success of the Civilian Conservation Corps, VISTA, and the Peace Corps, the idea of national service has also been linked to the proposal for universal military service. In the last few years, however, the concept of national service as an obligation for all has become separated from that of military service, although the latter could count as national service. In general, the military is confronted by a growing need for highly trained personnel. It needs recruits who have already achieved a level of school performance above that of the average young person from a low-income community. Thus, the military services, with their volunteer recruitment, are less and less interested in taking on the responsibility for socializing young people for the world of work.

National service could work without spending vast sums for training camps and salaries. The costs need not be much greater than those already entailed by job creation and training programs. The national-service requirement could be satisfied by any number of options for volunteer and paid work. Thus, for youth from low-income areas even summer youth employment could qualify as part of national service. For affluent young people, participation as volunteers or as counselors, trainers, and the like in community-based programs would also qualify for national-service credit.

Much more could be said about the potential and the problems of national service. The important point is that national service can grow out of sustained cooperative efforts to provide work and training. It would be better to allow a national-service system to grow out of the developing links between business, the schools, and local voluntary associations than to impose some system devised at the national level on states and communities throughout the United States.

However, the bleak situation of minority youth from low-income communities in the 1980s demands the kind of special attention that cannot wait for the eventual development of a comprehensive national-service system. Census figures show that despite major advances in the entry of blacks and Hispanics into professional and technical fields, the opportunity and income gaps between whites and nonwhites are widening. Median black income in 1980 was only 56 percent of that of whites. Among black families, 54 percent had household incomes below $15,000 a year, compared with 28 percent of white families. And these startling disparities are largely explained by the effects of birth into a female-headed family. In 1980 an estimated 47 percent of all black families with children were headed by women, and these families were almost twice as likely to be poor as families with a male wage earner present. Nor do the census figures offer any immediate hope for less educated black males. Between 1962 and 1980 the number of unemployed black men grew by 3.34 million while the number of employed black men increased by 1.79 million. Unless we redouble our efforts to reverse these trends, it is most likely that the generation of poor teenagers described in this volume will further swell the dependency rolls.

Policy pessimists are likely to argue that more federal spending will not reverse the growth of an "underclass" of chronically unemployed, predominantly minority people. Their claim is that policies that did not work in the past will not work now; besides, "ye have the poor always with you."

Perhaps. But the present situation in low-income areas would no doubt be even worse had it not been for important efforts made in the 1960s and 1970s in the areas of affirmative action, compensatory education, open admissions, employment training and subsidized work experiences, and sex education. The 1980 census shows, for example, that the median educational level of young blacks is now equal to that of whites, a direct result of years of public programs and countless policy initiatives at all levels of society. But the most recent data also show that a rising educational level among minority youth is a necessary but not sufficient answer to their employment and training problems. Blacks and other racial minorities in the United States continue to face greater obstacles to labor-force entry than do whites, a fact that has been documented in this study as well.

The young people whose voices are heard in this book are representative of low-income teenagers and young adults throughout the United States. The problems they face in gaining adequate education and early work experiences demand more than the substitution of federally subsidized work for jobs developed through the efforts of local business/public-sector partnerships. The policy direction in youth employment and training taken by the Reagan administration does involve private business to a degree not attained by past efforts, but the shortfall in job openings at the entry level and the decline in training and school-to-work programs appear to be accelerating with cuts in federal spending. Any lasting solution to the problems of low-income youth will require both the continuation of all existing efforts at local job creation and an increase in federally sponsored, competitively funded programs (based on proposals monitored at the federal level) to reach school dropouts and teenage parents. Annual funding levels of $5 billion or more for training and job creation are needed to supplement present efforts by local partnerships. The successful Urban Development Action Grants Program and the Youth Development Project demonstrations provided models for the targeting and selection of sound proposals for local action. What is lacking now is any national consensus that in the face of rising budget deficits there is nonetheless an urgent need to get on with the youth employment and training movement. And this lack of consensus is most unfortunate because it occurs at a time when manpower studies all show that significant progress could be achieved without disruptive costs. By the end of this decade the nation will very likely be facing labor shortages as the declining youth cohorts of the 1970s begin to enter the labor force. But this overall decline in the demand for entry-level jobs will not decrease among minority youth and white youth from low-income backgrounds. These youth populations will be in a position to benefit from demographic declines only if investments in their literacy and job skills are made now.

The past twenty years of policy initiatives show that we can prevent new generations of poor kids from ending up as street-corner men and bitter women, but this can happen only if we can marshal the resources and sustain the commitment over a period longer than a single presidential term. This book has shown that failure to maintain such a commitment to the nation's least advantaged youth will only produce higher rates of teenage pregnancy, more antisocial teenage behavior, and ever-increasing involvement of young people in the world of illegal hustles. Thus, as a nation we cannot afford to tolerate the growing sentiment that the situation of poor kids is someone else's problem. In truth, these are all our children.

Notes

1. Manpower Demonstration and Research Corporation, "Youth Incentive Entitlement Eligibility Survey" (New York, MDRC, 1980).

2. Berlin, Gordon and Joanne Duhl. "Education, Equity and Economic Excellence: The Critical Role of Second Chance Basic Skills and Job Training Programs" (New York: The Ford Foundation, 1984), p. 28.

3. Ginzberg, Eli. "The Job Problem," *Scientific American,* November 1977, Volume 237, Number 5, pp. 43–51.

Epilog: Three Years Later

Where are they now? An informal follow-up survey produced some rather surprising results, as well as some that were quite predictable. Here is a brief, but representative, sample.

Ruth P. of Zero, Mississippi, is a senior in college, where she is getting excellent grades. She has become active in local politics and hopes to go to law school.

Alain Cooper is a junior in college and still plans to become a doctor.

Darryl Conway has disappeared. As a middle-level dealer in the network headed by Nicky Barnes, he was forced to go underground when Barnes was arrested and turned informer. According to the kids at the candy store, there is a $50,000 contract on Darryl.

Biker, the Greenpoint boy who always wanted to operate machinery, drives a delivery truck and is thinking of joining the Merchant Marine. He has cut down on his criminal activity and makes extra money by re-modeling bars.

C.C. is still hanging out on the streets in Harlem. The street-corner boy is well on his way toward becoming a street-corner man, partly as a result of his long history of indulgence in angel dust.

Buster is still pursuing his career as an incompetent criminal, breaking into stores while high on Quaaludes, getting "busted," and being released to repeat the cycle.

Margo Sharp is engaged to be married and planning to move to an afflu-ent community on Long Island.

Dorothea Caddy, who was running a brothel in Meridian at the age of seventeen, subsequently spent some time in jail for petty theft. Since then she has completed her G.E.D., and she now works as a counselor at a vo-cational center.

Ray-Ray Southern of Meridian was a pimp and petty criminal when we knew him. Later he was convicted of stealing from his employer and was sentenced to a year in Parchman, a prison notorious for its wretched con-ditions. Upon his release he became a preacher in a local church.

Johnny Morales, formerly of the Cocaine City Boys and numerous other crews, is a vocational counselor for minority youth, helping them choose a college and apply for financial aid. Today Johnny wears a three-piece suit and brags about his $20,000-a-year salary.

Carol J. of Meridian was forced to drop out of school when her mother refused to take care of her baby any longer. She became estranged from her family, moved to Baltimore, and is looking for a job.

Pestac finished high school and has begun a course that will prepare her for a job as a typist. She is still seeing the father of her baby.

Carmen was unable to keep her apartment, so she moved in with her sister. She tried to finish high school but had to drop out after having a second child.

Appendix: Employing Disadvantaged Youth in Community Analysis

As an employment demonstration, our program trained and employed 86 disadvantaged youths between the ages of 14 and 20. The young people worked in seven communities in four cities. In each community they were trained in "world-of-work" skills—promptness, ability to meet deadlines, public speaking, resumé writing, and completion of employment forms. But this training was ancillary to the actual work each of them performed. Their jobs as "community research assistants" required extensive writing assignments, including life histories of themselves and their peers, interviews with their peers and parents, descriptions of their experiences in other employment situations, field notes about events in their neighborhoods, and evaluations of their experience in the demonstration itself. Those who performed these tasks well were given additional responsibilities in the recruitment and training of other assistants. Where possible, their employment on the demonstration lasted up to nine months. Young people who could not meet writing deadlines or otherwise demonstrate motivation to gain from their employment were terminated, generally after four to six weeks. Seventeen percent (that is, 13) of the young people we hired fell into this category.

As a youth employment program, this demonstration recapitulates many of the patterns of success and difficulty normally experienced by larger CETA-sponsored youth programs. Teenagers had to be helped with social security applications, working papers, school records, and check-cashing cards. Parents often had to be convinced that their children's employment would not lead to decreases in household benefits (AFDC, food stamps, etc.). It was necessary to establish standards of work and discipline in regular meetings with the young people in each community. Problems with delivery of checks and placement of new assistants on the payroll often led to frustration and initial hostility. Referrals of assistants to other jobs and occasional aid to youths who got into trouble in their neighborhoods were a constant source of extra work for the supervisors.

One of the strategies we used to develop the study might be called "ethnographic quota sampling." We selected the individuals to be studied in such a way as to establish "panels" of young people and adults who would represent the life patterns we wanted to learn about. The types of youth to be studied—and the choice of specific communities—were suggested by the policy issues to be addressed by the study. The issues were the following:

1. School dropouts and their experiences—how to communicate with and best recruit early school leavers for participation in job and educational programs.
2. Young mothers' work and family patterns—what are the special problems of young mothers and how can these best be accommodated in manpower programs?
3. Street life and crime—how do the opportunities for income generated by the street culture of urban areas influence youth participation in the regular economy and in educational programs?
4. Making it in the ghetto—who are the youth who achieve upward mobility despite the disadvantages of their social environment? How can this stream of youth maturing in low-income communities be supported and enlarged through public policy?
5. The manpower program experience—how do adolescents in disadvantaged areas experience manpower programs, and how are their attitudes and behaviors with regard to jobs and careers shaped by their experiences?
6. Alternative routes out of poverty—what are the various alternatives that young people contemplate and take in their search for routes out of poverty areas?
7. Youth as researchers and participants—what are the implications of employing adolescents to assist in the analysis of their communities both for the young people themselves and for the future of public policy and programs in their communities?
8. The role of community analysis in job programs—how can a program of direct observation be incorporated within traditional quantitative evaluation of policy and programs?

The way young people were recruited for the demonstration depended in large part on the issues that were being highlighted in each of the study communities. This emphasis, in turn, depended to some extent on the background that each field study director brought to the demonstration. Before turning to patterns of youth recruitment, therefore, we will look briefly at the way our field study directors were selected.

The overall goal of the demonstration was to work with young people in four cities to develop ethnographic accounts of the lives of disadvantaged youth in their community settings. The demonstration would base its findings on observations of the lives of adolescents rather than on quantitative survey questionnaires. As Robert Taggart, former administrator of the Office of Youth Programs, observes, "Unstructured interviews can yield greater insight into individuals and their motivations but are much more difficult to generalize. The quality of the insights depends on the degree of rapport, the continuity of observation and the understanding of the observer." The ethnographic approach relies on observations of life experiences rather than on questions about these experiences. Obviously, it is a more intensive approach, with the danger of overinvolvement ever present, but it is also the only way to put life experiences into their communal context.

In ethnographic community research, the desired outcome is a balanced picture of community life, especially as it bears on key issues, in this case the experiences of youth in the local economy. By selecting communities for study, rather than selecting a particular category of youth, it would be possible to sample the youth in each community to develop a representative picture of young people's experiences in different communities.

Since the research design also specified that the demonstration focus on some issues more intensely in a given community than in others, even though each community study would be as comprehensive as possible, the selection of field study directors in each location became a logical means toward determining how that emphasis should be developed. The issues we chose to specialize in for each community would arise in some part out of the particular skills and backgrounds of the field supervisors. At the same time, we would attempt to make each of the community studies as comprehensive as possible by selecting a diverse group of young people to work with in each city.

Ethnographic research is usually conducted by social scientists who have training at the doctoral level and beyond. Our intention, therefore, was to hire field study directors who had advanced graduate training and experience in ethnographic research. This presented no problem in the New York communities. The CUNY staff could draw upon the services of field study directors in Harlem, Greenpoint, and Williamsburg who not only had advanced training in ethnographic methods but were already conducting community studies in those areas. In Cleveland, Louisville, and Meridian, we had no such resources on which to draw. Delays in demonstration start-up through the summer and fall of 1979 (work began in the New York communities in July 1979 but could not begin in the other cities until the end of October of that year) increased the difficulty of recruiting trained ethnographers outside New York City before the beginning of the academic year. Academic ethnographers who might have been available either were reluctant to accept short-term positions or had no background of research or service in the communities in which we planned to work. This situation led us to recruit field study directors in Cleveland, Louisville, and Meridian who could make up for lack of academic training with depth of knowledge and service in those communities. The backgrounds of these individuals helped to define the issues emphasized in each community.

In each of the communities a period of intensive preliminary research preceded the actual selection of young people for employment in the demonstration. Before actual hiring, each of the demonstration staff members developed knowledge about the world of teenagers in specific neighborhoods within the study communities. Each field study director interviewed scores of teenagers and wrote field notes about the natural groupings of young people in those neighborhoods. In staff training sessions the characteristics of each of the neighborhoods and the backgrounds of all of the youths contacted there were reviewed.

The selection process whereby young people were placed on the demonstration payroll depended as much on the characteristics of the neighborhoods they would eventually write about as it did on features of their individual biographies. We sought to hire young people who would represent the various categories of disadvantaged youth—high achievers, street hustlers, teenage mothers, youth in manpower programs, and so on—but it was equally important that the young people selected be able to write about a large number of peers in neighborhoods that were representative of the social environments in which disadvantaged teenagers grow up. We needed a balance of neighborhood situations as much as we needed representativeness in individuals. Thus, in each city we selected some young people who came from public-housing projects and others who lived in lower-density neighborhoods of single-family or two-family homes. In Mississippi we also selected teenagers from some of the rural villages surrounding the small city of Meridian.

Young people who were representative of teenagers involved in the hustling life were selected from larger peer groups about which they could write. Thus, in Cleveland a young woman was hired who could write about life in an apartment building populated almost entirely by juveniles placed there by probation officers. In Harlem some youths were selected because they were members of different kinds of crews. The same considerations applied to young people selected from schools in the study communities. From each of the high schools or junior high schools where we recruited, an effort was made to select recognized high achievers, young people who had demonstrated promise but in some cases were not yet achieving up to their potential, as well as teenagers who were at risk of becoming dropouts owing to truancy and poor school performance.

None of the young people who eventually became our community research assistants were actually hired before they had completed an initial period of work without pay. When a particular teenager was selected by a field study director as a potential assistant, she or he was given a writing assignment and a deadline to meet. If the work came in more or less on time and the young person demonstrated real interest in the goals of the demonstration, another assignment was made with a similar deadline. If the work again came in at the designated time, the decision to hire was made. In making these assignments we were not interested in the young person's skills; no matter how poor they were at writing, we could work with them if they showed a desire to produce and a degree of interest in what we were doing that could sustain motivation.

Table A–1 summarizes the most important characteristics of the young people who took part in the demonstration as paid community research assistants. Of course, these figures bear no necessary relation to the actual demographics of disadvantaged youth in the communities we studied. Instead, they reflect the issues highlighted in specific communities. Thus, a disproportionate number of school dropouts were included in the Louisville panel; more younger teenagers were hired in Cleveland and New York; more teenage mothers were employed in the Meridian demonstration. And as noted earlier, about 80 percent of all the young demonstration workers were Afro-Americans. Although 86 teenagers were actually hired as community research assistants, the table reports on the backgrounds of 77 young people. The others were originally recruited as demonstration participants but soon were moved to clerical positions in which they assisted in the typing of field notes and office management even as they continued to write about their daily lives. Since these teenagers were not listed in the same personnel line as the community research assistants, their data do not appear in the table even though their backgrounds were quite similar to those of the assistants.

Table A–1
Characteristics of Community Research Assistants
(percent)

	New York N = 26	Cleveland N = 14	Louisville N = 18	Meridian N = 19	Total N = 77
Sex					
Male	61.5%	57.1%	44.4%	21.1%	46.7%
Female	38.5	42.8	55.6	78.9	53.3
Age					
14–16	26.9	28.6	—	5.3	15.6
17–18	46.2	35.7	27.8	57.9	42.8
19 +	26.9	35.9	72.2	36.8	41.6
Weeks Employed					
Less than 8	30.8	0.0	16.7	21.1	19.5
8–16	46.2	50.0	33.3	47.3	44.2
17–24	11.5	50.0	16.7	15.8	20.8
24 +	11.5	0.0	33.3	15.8	15.5
Education					
In school	61.5	64.3	27.8	57.9	53.3
Dropout	38.5	35.7	72.2	42.1	46.7

The community research assistants were employed for twenty hours per week at a wage of four dollars per hour. When some of them performed extremely well, their basic wage was raised by fifty cents per hour. The rationale for paying more than the minimum wage was the one so often voiced by employers in private business. We wanted our young workers to produce, and we wanted them to be motivated to do the best job they possibly could. Although one could have made these demands at the minimum wage, the higher rate had the psychological impact of justifying discipline. It made the young workers feel that they had found a good opportunity.

The training of the community research assistants began before their actual employment started. In fact, often there was no clear line between recruitment and training. The work assignments we offered were so out of the ordinary, so different from the work opportunities young people ordinarily encounter, that weeks of discussion might be required before some of the teenagers understood what was being asked of them.

Young people involved in petty hustles were generally wary of the proposition that they write about their lives and those of their friends on the streets. Before they would seriously consider the possibility of putting their thoughts and experiences on paper or, worse yet, writing about their friends, they had to be convinced that the adults involved in the demonstration were "cool." Months of hanging out were sometimes required before we could begin to describe the goals of the demonstration research. Wherever our field study director had worked with particular groups of street youth, trust that had been developed in the past could be called upon to assure troubled young people that their descriptions of illegal activities would not be used against them. In developing knowledge about youth in the upper reaches of the illegal economy, Terry Williams, who was responsible for much of the field research in this area, had to carefully cultivate relationships with young people who appeared to have the insight to systematically observe and reflect on their illegal activities.

Once trust had been established, the teenagers whom we wanted to recruit were asked to write a biography for which they would be paid a fixed fee. When the assignment came in as agreed upon, we would work with the teenager to improve the quality of his or her writing. At the same time, we would gradually reveal the purpose of the work. But in the majority of cases the written work was not forthcoming. For many reasons, the prospect of writing about their lives was too threatening for youths engaged in street hustles. In these cases we generally continued to conduct field work with these young people and their peers without actually placing them on our payroll.

Teenagers who were enrolled in school or work in private-sector jobs or manpower programs tended to perceive the demonstration as a possible windfall. To be paid up to eighty dollars per week for simply attending group meetings three times a week and doing some writing about life in their neighborhoods sounded too good to be true. Thus, whenever we described our work in school settings or to community groups we were besieged with informal applications for employment. In discussion meetings to which potential research assistants were invited, we had the opportunity to listen to young people as they described their activities and their everyday lives. The meetings also allowed us to learn about the current status of individuals. Were they working? Did they have a child? What was their situation with regard to school and family? Who were the adults who influenced them? And by what criteria could they be considered "disadvantaged"? With this information we could decide which of the hundreds of deserving young people we screened could best represent a particular segment of disadvantaged youth on our demonstration study teams.

Once the demonstration study teams had been formed and were functioning in each city, training sessions were held two or three times a week from January through September of 1980. In addition to the regular training sessions, the field study directors held regular meetings with individual community research assistants to discuss issues emerging from the writing that could not be brought to the full team.

The assignments given to the community research assistants always revolved around writing, but the content of the writing was quite varied. All of the young people were started off with biographical writing even before they began to be paid for their work on the demonstration. Once they had been hired, the assignments became more ambitious. The life histories had to be made more detailed, and when those details touched on the activities of peers we made further assignments that required the assistants to write about their friends' lives. Each assistant was also required to produce a map of his or her immediate neighborhood. From these maps we located the places where teenagers congregate. The maps also made the young people more aware of their physical surroundings. With the aid of the maps and the notations on them, we were better able to guide the observations and interviews that each assistant was required to conduct. At every training session we spent time teaching techniques of observing, interviewing, and above all, writing up these experiences.

Each community research assistant was given a writing quota based on individual ability. A dropout who has not been in school for a year or more may spend two hours writing a single page of a life history or a description of a group of friends. High achievers may be able to write three or four times as much in the same amount of time. These differences in ability naturally made it necessary for us to gear our demands to individual skill levels and to continually increase those demands as skills improved.

In each community the field study directors filled in details missing from the written materials through group discussions and interviews in the neighborhoods or with the community research assistants. These techniques produced solid ethnographic material on the relative proportions of young people involved in different adolescent lifestyles in the neighborhoods under study. A product of all the demonstration research was the development of networks of information and knowledge through which the young people in each of the neighborhoods could be not only interviewed but actually followed through a year of their lives. If a young person achieved special success in school or elsewhere in the community, our study teams heard about it. They also heard about troubles in the teenagers' families, scrapes with the law, attempts to get straight, and difficulties with lovers and children. So the actual written material produced by the young research assistants was not merely the product of their employment but an extensive set of documents from which we could draw additional knowledge.

In each of the communities in which the demonstration was conducted we can point to major successes with troubled teenagers. In Harlem, for example, one need only look at the experience of Neil Davis, a strapping, handsome 19-year-old who had high test scores but was writing at about the fourth-grade level and had serious problems with self-expression. The day after he joined the demonstration on a probationary basis he was jumped by three boys near his school. In the ensuing fight Neil was stabbed in the side with an ice pick; he spent two days in the hospital. After five months as a community research assistant, Neil's writing skills had improved by about two grade levels—a rapid gain perhaps, though not enough to bring him up to where he should be—but his behavior had changed drastically. He stayed out of fights throughout the academic year. To his teachers' surprise and delight he wore a jacket to school every day for most of the year, and although his work in English was still inadequate to allow him to pass the citywide comprehensive examination, he was much less threatened by writing and was able to accept teaching as he had never before been able to do.

Other teenagers managed to reenroll in school or G.E.D. programs. A few secured jobs that permitted them to get off welfare. All showed improved achievement in school. Unfortunately, we have no data for subsequent years because we were not funded to carry out any systematic follow-up after December 31, 1980.

About the Authors

Terry M. Williams is a senior research associate in sociology at the Graduate School and University Center, City University of New York. Born in McComb, Mississippi, he left at sixteen for New York City, where he now resides. He received his B.A. degree from Richmond College in 1972. He holds a Ph.D. in sociology from the City University of New York Graduate School. His fellowships include a National Institute on Drug Abuse Research Fellowship, an Operation Crossroads Africa Scholarship, a National Science Foundation Award, and a postdoctoral fellowship in behavioral research in drug abuse.

William Kornblum is a professor of sociology at the Graduate School and University Center of the City University of New York. A native of New York City, he received his doctorate from the University of Chicago in 1971. He is a specialist in community and urban studies, the author of *Blue Collar Community* (University of Chicago Press, 1974), and a frequent contributor to journals and magazines in the social sciences. Recent articles of his have appeared in *Dissent, Social Policy*, and *The Sciences*. Since 1973 he has also directed a research unit of the National Park Service housed at the CUNY Graduate School.